50 Activities for the International Chinese Classroom

Dongdong Chen
Cynthia W. Fellows

外语教学与研究出版社
FOREIGN LANGUAGE TEACHING AND RESEARCH PRESS
北京 BEIJING

Preface

It is a sincere honor to have the privilege of offering this preface to *50 Activities for the International Chinese Classroom*, authored by Chen Dongdong and Cynthia W. Fellows of Seton Hall University. What you find before you is a set of language "games" that are "serious"—in that they address a serious challenge, namely that of learning Chinese—and yet "fun" for both students and teachers.

I believe that Dr. Chen and Ms. Fellows are providing, for the first time, a set of instructional materials firmly grounded in what one of the 20th century pioneers in the field of Chinese language pedagogy, the late Dr. A. Ronald Walton, termed "the expertise base of the field" (Walton, 1996). In their introduction to this volume, Chen and Fellows explicitly state that the rationale for their book is "based on current cognitive research." Over 20 years ago, Walton (1996) stated that what was most lacking in all aspects of Chinese language learning and teaching at the time, including instructional materials, was the "transmission of expertise" in the form of a "chain... from disciplines...such as cognition...". This book is an important step in fulfilling that long-unmet need.

As I have had the genuine pleasure over the past several months of reading through Dongdong and Cynthia's manuscript, I cannot help but remember an early Sunday afternoon in March thirty years ago, when I found myself sitting at the dining room table in the home of my then-faculty advisor at Ohio State University, Dr. Timothy Light. Seated across from me was Dr. Tao-chung Yao.

At first glance, as then only potential collaborative writing partners, we could not have been more poorly matched. Ted (Tao-chung Yao's nickname) had already displayed his natural skills as a superb Chinese language teacher, with nearly a decade of classroom-based experience, and he had earned his master's degree in Chinese philosophy at Seton Hall University and a Ph.D. in history on a study of a Taoist sect during the Yuan dynasty at the University of Arizona. As for me, I was two quarters into my Chinese language teaching career as a Ph.D. student at OSU, with a declared scholarly interest in modern Chinese syntax and pragmatics, and a still-lingering love of the performing arts from my drama major days at Kenyon College in the 1970s.

For whatever reason—instinct, intuition, or sheer luck—Tim (Dr. Timothy Light's nickname) had somehow thought that the two of us would make a good team to bring to fruition a project that Ted had been working on in a piecemeal manner for a number of years. (Tim also had the ulterior motive of having to leave town earlier that Sunday morning on a business trip, and wondered if I would be willing to give Ted a lift to Port Columbus International Airport for his plane flight home to Massachusetts!) In any event, I found myself moving a bit closer to Ted's chair to look at the five sheets of Chinese manuscript he had spread out on that dining room table. Those five sheets of paper eventually became the anchoring initial pages of *Let's Play Games in Chinese*, what we then more simply dubbed "Games for Learning Chinese."

In the course of reading Dongdong and Cynthia's manuscript, I have been constantly reminded that the same sort of seeming "incompatibility" that did not keep Tim from bringing Ted and me together in 1986 is what makes this new volume such a logical successor to—and indeed, improvement on—what Ted and I did back in the previous century. Like Ted and me, Dongdong and Cynthia bring together two very different linguistic and cultural backgrounds, as well as the two most important skills necessary for the best possible Chinese (or any) language teaching team, namely, Dongdong's intuitive, native understanding of the Chinese language, and Cynthia's experiential foundation of what it takes to be a successful learner of Chinese as a second or foreign language.

Three decades later, we are enriched and informed by illuminating new theoretical models such as intercultural communication, and practical tools reflected in the ever-evolving and -maturing fields of instructional and learning technology. Dongdong and Cynthia have both embraced and incorporated such scholarly and technological enhancements, as well as maintaining elements that Ted and I felt in 1986 would make our volume at once both pedagogically and practically sound—namely:

- Recognizing American's affection for games as manifested in living rooms throughout the United States and viewed on American television—in Ted's and my book, *Bingo* and *Concentration* (both still a part of this book), and in the current volume, *Clue*® and *Jeopardy*®.

- A thoroughly inconceivable (in Ted's and my time) technological range of possibilities—note that I composed the English manuscript for *Let's Play Games in Chinese* on a Smith-Corona electric typewriter, even while Ted was blazing a CAI trail as being one of the first two people in the Chinese language teaching profession in the United States to pioneer the use of Hypercard character flashcard programs on Macintosh platforms in 1984. I envy the references to WeChat and iTranslate in Dongdong and Cynthia's volume.

- Enriching the range of game options in terms of both proficiency levels and learning settings, including settings outside the language classroom for multi-week learning plans—in the former regard, echoing what one of my colleagues from the Washington, D.C. area, Heidi Byrnes of Georgetown University, first characterized as a lifelong language learning profile of "literature from the beginning, language to the end" (personal communication, cited in Phillips, 1999), but what I prefer to call "culture from the beginning and language to the end."

- A far more rich, robust, and theoretically informed framing mechanism of "Focus" prefaces for each and every game.

- And most important, as the authors of the current volume note, "to keep things fresh for ourselves and our students"—consistent with the words of Tim Light in his introduction to our volume assessing what we were attempting to do, namely, "[to] provide materials and inspiration for getting language out of the book...and *into* real use in a setting that is *fun*" (cited in the introduction of the book, *Let's Play Games in Chinese*, 2002).

In sum, while we sadly lost Ted last year, I am confident that I can speak for him in saying that *50 Activities for the International Chinese Classroom* is more than a worthy successor to our humble, *paozhuan-yinyu* pedagogical "tradition" of *Let's Play Games in Chinese*. And on behalf of Ted, let me say once again, let the games begin!

Scott McGinnis[*]

Silver Spring, Maryland

October 16, 2016

---

[*] Scott McGinnis is a professor at the Defense Language Institute, USA, and an associate editor of the *Chinese as a Second Language* (CLTA).

References

Phillips, J. Introduction: Standards for World Languages—On a Firm Foundation. In J. Phillips & R. Terry (eds.). *Foreign Language Standards: Linking Research, Theories, and Practices*. Lincolnwood, IL: National Textbook Company, 1999.

Walton, A. R. Reinventing Language Fields: The Chinese Case. In S. McGinnis (ed.). *Chinese Pedagogy: An Emerging Field*. Columbus: Ohio State University Foreign Language Publications, 1996.

Yao, T. & McGinnis, S. *Let's Play Games in Chinese*. Boston: Cheng & Tsui Company, 2002.

Introduction

50 Activities for the International Chinese Classroom presents an innovative approach to the learning of Chinese along the lines of Communicative Language Teaching (CLT). The ideas of CLT—creating a friendly and supportive student-centered learning environment with meaningful contexts in order to develop communicative competence—have been widely implemented in the teaching of mainstream foreign languages, but less enthusiastically or even reluctantly used in Chinese teaching. Therefore, promoting communicative Chinese teaching through activities is the first goal of this book.

All foreign language teachers must face the following challenges: arousing learners' interest, motivating students to learn, and helping them retain what has been learned. Chinese language teachers, however, are faced with an additional challenge—the difficulty of the language itself. What can we teachers do to make learning Chinese less of a struggle and more of a gratifying adventure for our students? And since far too many Chinese language learners give up on their studies, how can we maintain students' interest throughout the long journey to communicative competence?

This book is aimed at addressing these questions *practically* by providing meaningful and engaging classroom activities that specifically target the unique linguistic features of Chinese which pose such a challenge for English-speaking learners; for instance, tones, characters, unique grammatical structures, etc. Our rationale, based on current cognitive research, is three-fold.

- **SPACED-REPETITION**

Just as cramming does not work for students in the long-term, neither does it work if it is the teacher who is doing the "cramming" in the classroom. Covering material in a concentrated fashion hoping that mastery will ensue is counter-productive. To truly learn, our brains need both a rest period of non-exposure, *and then* need to be called upon later to recall. In other words, the brain needs practice retrieving partially learned material before it can be truly considered mastered. While the ideal amount of time in between recall sessions varies depending upon the circumstances and individual, teachers should plan on spacing out their coverage of certain topics over time. As learning is not accomplished in one fell swoop, activities are a needed addition to formal teaching, exercises, and testing. For the purpose of spaced-repetition, we have created two different activities for each particular linguistic item.

- **VARIETY IS THE SPICE OF LIFE—AND LEARNING**

With spaced-repetition being so important, variety becomes necessary. Asking for recall in different contexts makes learning more memorable and thus more effective. Variety is also necessary because as we all know what works for one student may not work as well for another. This is also true for teachers. While many teachers will have excellent results with competitive games, other teachers might struggle to get the students engaged if they themselves see games as silly time-wasters. In order to be an effective teacher, one must be true to one's personality. Using a medley of different types of activities thus substantially increases the odds of successful teaching and learning.

- **SUPPORTIVE LEARNING ENVIRONMENT**

And on that note, personalities matter in any classroom, but perhaps no more so than in the *foreign-language* classroom. Since language is the means by which we all express ourselves, egos tend to be fragile when faced with the inability to be our true selves. By their very nature, activities create a supportive, convivial classroom atmosphere which increases the intrinsic motivation of students so they are more apt to carry on in their studies.

We see this book being used in several ways. First, teachers can simply use the activities in their own classrooms as is. Knowing how preparation and small details dictate an activity's success or failure, care has been taken to illustrate the procedures step-by-step. Second, we hope that these activities will inspire teachers to develop or improve upon their own activities. As teachers, we can all use some new tricks of the trade to keep things fresh for ourselves and our students. And, thirdly, the activities can be used as an emergency remedy. Let's say you or a previous teacher has taught your students the bǎ structure, but one day you notice that the students seem rusty. That would be an excellent time to look for an activity to bring that structure back to the forefront of their brains.

All in all, it is the authors' hope that Chinese language teachers—from novice to experienced—find this book a handy and effective tool in their teaching toolbox.

The Authors

Seton Hall University

February, 2016

Acknowledgments

We would like to thank all our students who have unknowingly inspired us to create and then fine-tune our classroom activities over the years. Their enthusiasm and above all their progress were the catalyst for the development and completion of this book. In addition, special thanks to the following Chinese teachers: Zhao Yanfei for reviewing the Chinese manuscript; Yong Ho, Mei Zhao, Miao-Fen Tseng, Marisa Fang and Xia Liang for providing such valuable suggestions.

Contents

Chapter 5: Internalizing Grammar II / 81

Chapter 6: Putting It All Together / 130

References and Further Readings / 149

Chapter 1
Making Tones Accurate

In this chapter we target three aspects of *pinyin*: producing *pinyin*, recognizing and deciphering *pinyin*, and the challenges of *pinyin*. Six activities were developed—two for each aspect—as shown below:

1 **Otherwise Known As**

2 **Sound & Tone Pair-up**

3 **Sounds Around the World**

4 **"Copy That" Contest**

5 **"Odd" Tone Out**

6 **Race to *Pinyin* Perfection**

Otherwise Known As

FOCUS This activity is useful as an ice-breaker while further practicing tying together pronunciation with tones in the early days of a class.

LEVEL Elementary ★ ☆ ☆   **TIME** 5—10 minutes

PROCEDURE

01 Using long thin sheets of paper, the teacher writes each student's Chinese name in *pinyin* on one end of a sheet, and his or her English name on the other end. There should be as many sheets of paper as there are students.

02 Depending upon the size of the paper used, either roll each of the papers up as in a scroll or put them in an envelope.

03 Write the following on the board and have the class read it out loud a couple of times. To illustrate, the teacher should first substitute his or her own name for "X".

> X shì shéi?
> X shì wǒ/nǐ/tā.

04 Now have a student select a piece of paper. They are to ask the question by substituting the Chinese name written down on the paper for "X". The student who has that Chinese name should respond by saying "X shì wǒ" and take the piece of paper. That same student should now select a piece of paper and follow the same pattern. This continues until all students have their own names before them.

05 Afterwards, the teacher can randomly select a student's name and while showing the piece of paper ask, "X shì shéi?" Students who remember who "X" is should point and say, "X shì tā." Or, if sitting close by, should say, "X shì nǐ."

NOTE

For this activity, each student not only needs a Chinese name but also must be familiar enough with it beforehand to recognize it when it is said. If teachers do not have time to think of a Chinese name for each student, they can have the students use a Chinese naming tool, such as http://www.mandarintools.com/chinesename.html, and then polish the names for more authenticity.

ACTIVITY

2) **Sound & Tone Pair-up**

FOCUS This activity focuses on catching trouble spots early on. And, not just the obvious ones. Since it is increasingly common to have students with different mother tongues and backgrounds in one classroom, this activity takes into account each student's personal difficulties.

LEVEL Elementary ★ ☆ ☆ 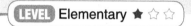   **TIME** 15 minutes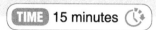

PROCEDURE

01 In preparation, the teacher writes down the specific initials, finals and tones that their students are having difficulty with. Choose ten words or phrases that contain those sounds and tones. Try to choose words that are related to the lives of your students or are characteristic of Chinese culture. For example:

- Xiǎo Zhào (little Zhao)

- zǎochen (morning)

- qǐchuáng yǐhòu (after getting up)

- chī ròubāozi (eat pork buns)

- hē dòujiāng (drink soy milk)

- bēizhe shūbāo (carrying a bookbag)

- qíchē shàngxué (ride a bicycle to school)

- ránhòu (then)

- jiàndào (see)

- lǎoshī hé tóngxué (teachers and classmates)

02 The teacher then gives each student six index cards on which the students are to write down the two initials, two finals, and two tones that they personally have the most difficulty with. While the students are doing this, walk around the room, jot down any sounds or tones the students have chosen that you have not anticipated and adjust your list accordingly.

03 When the students are done, the teacher reads the syllables which contain elements that the students are struggling with, one at a time. If a student has written down either an initial, final or tone which is contained in that word, they are to raise their card.

04 Then the teacher reads these syllables or words one by one again, and the student who has the initial, final or tone in that syllable or word should match up with other students who have written down an initial, final or tone that would make the complete word. For example, if the word is "xiǎo", a student who has written "x" matches up with students who have written "iao" and the third tone " ˇ ".

NOTE

Since it is plausible that not all the initials and finals that form useful words will be written down by the students, the teacher should have on stand-by any initials and finals that would be necessary to form the words on the list. For example, the teacher would prepare z, ch, en, and ao to form "zǎochen" when combined with a student's third tone.

ACTIVITY 3

Sounds Around the World

FOCUS Students who choose to study Chinese are typically curious about the world at large. This activity uses that curiosity to hold the students' interest in what otherwise would be the mundane task of practicing *pinyin*.

 **LEVEL** Elementary ★ ☆ ☆    **TIME** 15 minutes

PROCEDURE

01 In advance, the teacher prepares the following:

- One handout that contains two separate lists: one for city names and the other for the countries to which those cities belong. While making the lists, try to include the names of the cities and countries where your students come from. *(See Sample A and Sample B.)*

- Two worksheets which ask the students where particular cities are located. In addition, each worksheet provides the "answers" for the questions asked on the worksheet. *(See Exercise A, Exercise B, Answer A and Answer B.)*

02 The teacher and the class first read all the city and country names out loud together. This functions as an excellent warm-up for the students' mouths and is a good time to introduce some of the meanings behind the names, as well as answer any questions.

03 Divide the students into pairs. Hand out the worksheets, giving a different worksheet to each member within a pair.

04 The student with "Exercise A" asks the first question. The student with "Exercise B" then gives the answer by looking at the "answers" provided at the bottom of "Exercise B". After the student with "Exercise A" fills in the answer, it is now time for the student with "Worksheet B" to ask a question, and so forth.

05 When the students have finished, the teacher leads the class in reading out loud all the city and country names one more time while reminding students to pay attention to *pinyin*. If there is extra time, the teacher can check the students' comprehension of the English equivalents by using globes and/or maps.

Sample A

城市	拼音	英文
西安	Xī'ān	Xi'an
上海	Shànghǎi	Shanghai
香港	Xiānggǎng	Hong Kong
纽约	Niǔyuē	New York
芝加哥	Zhījiāgē	Chicago
华盛顿	Huáshèngdùn	Washington
波士顿	Bōshìdùn	Boston
东京	Dōngjīng	Tokyo
巴黎	Bālí	Paris
伦敦	Lúndūn	London
罗马	Luómǎ	Rome
柏林	Bólín	Berlin
巴塞罗那	Bāsàiluónà	Barcelona
莫斯科	Mòsīkē	Moscow
悉尼	Xīní	Sydney
多伦多	Duōlúnduō	Toronto

Sample B

国家	拼音	英文
中国	Zhōngguó	China
美国	Měiguó	America (USA)
日本	Rìběn	Japan
法国	Fǎguó	France

(Continued table)

国家	拼音	英文
英国	Yīngguó	England
意大利	Yìdàlì	Italy
德国	Déguó	Germany
西班牙	Xībānyá	Spain
俄罗斯	Éluósī	Russia
澳大利亚	Àodàlìyà	Australia
加拿大	Jiānádà	Canada

Exercise A

问题 （城市）+ 在 + 哪儿？　　　北京在哪儿？ Where is Beijing?

回答 （城市）+ 在 +（国家）。　北京在中国。 Beijing is in China.

1.　问题：西安在哪儿？
　　回答：西安在_____。

2.　问题：纽约在哪儿？
　　回答：纽约在_____。

3.　问题：华盛顿在哪儿？
　　回答：华盛顿在_____。

4.　问题：东京在哪儿？
　　回答：东京在_____。

5.　问题：伦敦在哪儿？
　　回答：伦敦在_____。

6.　问题：柏林在哪儿？
　　回答：柏林在_____。

7.　问题：巴塞罗那在哪儿？
　　回答：巴塞罗那在_____。

8.　问题：多伦多在哪儿？
　　回答：多伦多在_____。

Answer B

城市	所在的国家
上海，香港	中国
芝加哥，波士顿	美国
巴黎	法国
罗马	意大利
莫斯科	俄罗斯
悉尼	澳大利亚

問題 （城市）+ 在 + 哪儿?　　　北京在哪儿？ Where is Beijing?

回答 （城市）+ 在 +（国家）。　　北京在中国。 Beijing is in China.

1. 问题：上海在哪儿?
   回答：上海在_____。

2. 问题：香港在哪儿?
   回答：香港在_____。

3. 问题：芝加哥在哪儿?
   回答：芝加哥在_____。

4. 问题：波士顿在哪儿?
   回答：波士顿在_____。

5. 问题：巴黎在哪儿?
   回答：巴黎在_____。

6. 问题：罗马在哪儿?
   回答：罗马在_____。

7. 问题：莫斯科在哪儿?
   回答：莫斯科在_____。

8. 问题：悉尼在哪儿?
   回答：悉尼在_____。

Answer A

城市	所在的国家
西安	中国
纽约，华盛顿	美国
东京	日本
伦敦	英国
柏林	德国
巴塞罗那	西班牙
多伦多	加拿大

"Copy That" Contest

FOCUS Achieving accurate Chinese pronunciation is a lengthy process which occurs over the course of a learner's studies. While it may be tempting to have students run through seemingly endless practice sessions of individual *pinyin*, doing so does little to help students fine-tune their speech. Not only do most students find this sort of practice boring and frustrating (in any language, mind you), but, more importantly, this sort of untethered practice rarely transfers over to real speech. One needs context to learn effectively. In other words, teachers must provide students with meaningful content to mimic. By using a "top-down approach" where whole lines and sentences receive top priority, any subsequent practice and correction by the teacher becomes all the more effective.

LEVEL Intermediate—Advanced ☆ ★ ★

TIME A month-long project with roughly 10—15 minutes per class period twice a week, concluding with a speech contest.

PROCEDURE

There are two versions of this activity: one where students mimic accurate pronunciation through concentrated practice, and the other where students fine-tune their pronunciation via mimicking natural dialogues. In both versions, the content, once explained by the teacher, is truly meaningful to the students and becomes more so over the course of practicing.

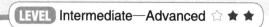

— Individual Competition —

Poetry recitation is a time-proven technique for improving one's language skills. While memorizing and reciting poetry has unfortunately fallen by the wayside in the West, it would be a shame for students not to have this valuable experience at least once during their educational experience. Since today's students often suffer from difficulty concentrating, poetry recitation shows them the joy in training their brains to slow down and focus on one thing. Additionally, there truly is no better way to appreciate one of the highest art forms that Chinese culture has to offer. Translations of Chinese poetry, while admirable, just do not capture the simple profundity of Chinese classical poetry.

01 In preparation, the teacher carefully selects several poems from which the students can choose from. The elegance and simplicity of Tang dynasty poems makes them particularly suitable for intermediate Chinese language learners. Be sure to select poems which contain mostly characters that the students will recognize. Then create individual handouts for each poem which has *pinyin* on top of each character.

02 Over the course of several weeks, introduce the poems. Be sure to cover no more than one poem per class period. Go over each poem's meaning by using easy-to-understand Chinese, hand gestures, and body movements. Finish up by reading the poem together as a class.

03 After all the poems have been introduced, have each student select their individual poem. Having two or more students pick the same poem is quite effective learning reinforcement. In most cases one or two students will really take to Chinese poetry, so by all means give the students the option to search around and choose a poem that you have not gone over in class.

04 Scour the web for good video examples of Chinese people reciting the poems that have been chosen and send the links to the students.

05 As the contest date approaches, have the students practice at least once before the class for a quiz grade.

—— Group Competition ——

As students progress, mimicking natural speech, with all the attendant emotive impact, becomes a possibility—and an exciting challenge for students.

01 The teacher carefully selects scenes from Chinese movies and television serials that not only can stand on their own without having to watch the entire movie, but whose dialogues contain valuable vocabulary and sentence structures for the students to learn. Three to five minutes is a good length. Then create an individual handout for each scene with *pinyin* and an annotated transcription of the dialogue.

02 The teacher then divides the class into groups based on the selected movie clips and assigns the roles. Be sure to give sufficient thought to group dynamics and each individual student's ability when assigning both groups and roles.

03 Take time from one or two class periods to watch the movie clips and go over sentence structures. Afterwards, send the students links to the video clips.

04 For the remainder of the time before the competition, devote some class time for the students to practice their scenes. Have them begin by first reading their roles correctly and then progress to reciting their roles without the script.

NOTE

While holding a speech contest at the end is not absolutely necessary, the pressure of public performances does have a way of encouraging students to work harder than they normally would.

ACTIVITY

5 "Odd" Tone Out

FOCUS Choral reading is often considered an out-of-date pedagogical tool in many Western societies today. Criticism that reading out loud in unison interferes with students' comprehension is indeed legitimate. However, once comprehension is attained, choral reading can attune students to a language's unique stresses and rhythms. Needless to say, a tonal language like Chinese is particularly suited for choral reading. Yet no matter how effective choral reading is in this regard, Western students are often initially resistant to it. This activity overcomes that resistance by giving students a challenge—to listen and find the teacher's errors.

LEVEL Elementary—Intermediate ★ ★ ☆   **TIME** 5—10 minutes

PROCEDURE

01 The teacher selects a text that is slightly beneath the students' level. For this activity to work well, the students must be able to readily grasp the meaning of the text with very little help from the teacher. The text should be simple enough that the students' brains can almost solely focus on the tones and rhythm of the text, but not so simple as to seem childish.

02 After handing out the text or writing it on the board, have the students silently read it to themselves. After a quick check that everyone understands the text's meaning, the teacher and the class start to read it out loud in unison.

03 Once you have read it out loud together once—or at most, twice—tell the students, from the next round onward you will deliberately say a few tones incorrectly. For instance, you might mispronounce "都" by saying "dǒu". Their job is to catch you when you make an error by raising their hands and stating what your mistake was.

04 In subsequent rounds, by all means let a few brave students take on your role of misspeaking.

NOTE

Some Western students who are unaccustomed to repetitive chanting might find doing this a bit odd. Acknowledge their viewpoint and then ask them to pretend that they are in China. Showing a video of Chinese students in school will show them what they have missed out on—or have not been subjected to—depending on one's perspective.

ACTIVITY

6

Race to *Pinyin* Perfection

FOCUS Learning *pinyin* does not stop after the introductory level. By dint of not being in a daily environment surrounded by the sounds of Chinese, students must make a concerted effort to remember the *pinyin* for each and every word they learn. Moreover, as students' vocabulary builds, it is far too easy for students—regardless of location—to become confused with all the homophones that differ only in tone. Hence, continued practice is of great use for students.

LEVEL Elementary—Advanced ★ ★ ★   **TIME** 5—10 minutes

PROCEDURE

There is really little, if any, preparation for this activity. The teacher will be dictating sentences which are either made on the fly, quickly prepared in advance, or taken from previous lessons. Whichever way, the sentences should reinforce previously learned sentence structures and vocabulary.

01 Divide the class into two to four teams depending upon the size of the board. One student from each team goes to the board. After the teacher dictates a sentence, the students are to write the *pinyin* on the board.

02 The odds are that there will be errors—including that of *pinyin*. The students' teammates then have to fix the errors. Be sure to give hints to the students on what is wrong.

03 The first team to have a perfectly written sentence—with correct tones— wins a point.

NOTE

01 Due to its short nature and little required preparation, this activity is ideal to use when a lesson runs shorter than expected or when, after a particularly hard lesson, the class could use a little pick-me-up.

02 This activity can get a bit chaotic as students tend to huddle around the board to try and fix the errors while others are calling out "Fix this!" or "Fix that!" As long as everyone is engaged, don't worry about maintaining order.

Chapter 2

Mastering Characters

In this chapter we focus on three different features regarding characters: the logic of Chinese characters, stroke order and muscle memory, and analyzing characters. Again, with two activities for each, six are presented in total. They are:

7 Chinese Building Blocks

8 Picture This

9 Writers with a Deadline

10 Air-Writing Characters

11 Root Search

12 Look It Up, Fast!

Chinese Building Blocks

FOCUS This activity is a first step in students' journey to unlocking the logic puzzle that is Chinese. Encouraging them to see the individual components within characters early on helps create good mental habits that will quicken their progress in the long run and more importantly enhance their enjoyment of Chinese.

LEVEL Elementary ★ ☆ ☆

TIME In-Class Discussion: 10—15 minutes each
Homework: N/A

PROCEDURE

01 Illustrate to the class the modular nature of Chinese characters and the ways in which radicals, the component parts of characters, are shuffled around to create new words. Show examples of how, while some characters only contain a single radical (such as 人 and 土), the majority of Chinese characters contain two or three radicals arranged in various ways, as in 你 and 学 .

02 For homework, give the students a worksheet which asks them to write out as many characters as possible for each of the different types of character formation. Encourage students to use a dictionary and, of course, their textbooks. *(See Sample.)*

03 Discuss their answers in the next class. Be sure to highlight practical words, as well as those which are impractical at this point in their studies, yet still interesting.

Ask the students to examine their own Chinese names in terms of radical composition.

Sample

单个部件	左右结构	上下结构	左中右结构	上中下结构	半包围结构	全包围结构	"品"字结构	……

| 人 | 你 | 学 | 谢 | 茶 | 区 | 回 | 品 | |

Picture This

FOCUS From their first day of their first Chinese language class, students are aware of the pictorial nature of Chinese characters. But somehow during the learning process, students often lose sight of this, which is a shame since the visual nature of Chinese is one of the main attractions of the language. As such, be sure to take time in class to stop and "enjoy" the characters through casual mentions and through activities such as the following. Doing so will not only pique students' interest, but also provide helpful mnemonic imagery that facilitates learning.

LEVEL Elementary—Advanced ★ ★ ★

TIME Preliminary Demonstration: 10 minutes
Homework: N/A
Guessing Game: 20 minutes

PROCEDURE

01 The teacher selects characters in advance that the students have studied before—and that can be easily, or somewhat easily, described verbally or pictorially. There should be one character for each student. Write each of these characters on its own index card.

02 By this point, your students are undoubtedly already aware of the pictorial nature of Chinese characters, so jump right in. Tell the students that you are going to describe a character and they are to guess which character you are describing. For example, for 从 you might say, "One person walks ahead, and the other follows." The students should hopefully be able to guess 从. As this is not easy for non-native speakers, be patient. Describe another character for them to guess, but this time draw a simple picture.

For example, for 梦 , you could draw a boy sleeping against a tree, under the stars, and with beautiful thoughts in his head.

03 Now tell the students that they will be selecting an index card with a character on it. They are to look at the component parts within it, and describe it in such a way that their classmates can guess which character it is. They can do this either verbally or pictorially—or both. Give the students a week to complete the homework assignment. As this can be a challenging assignment, be sure to give plenty of guidance and check up on their progress throughout the week.

04 Since you have been giving assistance all along, all should be well and good enough to do the guessing part of the activity after you hand their papers back. If not, give the students a day or two to digest your comments before having other students try to guess the characters.

05 The final part of the activity is simply having students come up, one at a time, to present their descriptions for their classmates to guess. Be prepared to give further clues if the students are stuck.

Writers with a Deadline

FOCUS While there is some debate among Chinese native speakers on the importance of stroke order, helping foreign learners of Chinese to get the stroke order more or less right in the beginning will help them in two ways. First, it will make writing Chinese more comfortable for them and thereby increase their writing speed. Secondly, a solid knowledge of stroke order will enable them to decipher Chinese handwriting and varying typefaces with greater success. This activity helps students make the necessary self-corrections in their own writing.

LEVEL Elementary ★ ☆ ☆   **TIME** 20—25 minutes

PROCEDURE

01 Prepare an eight-column worksheet with a sample two- to nine-stroke character at the top of each column. *(See Sample.)*

02 Working in pairs, have the students race to write in as many characters as possible that contain the required number of strokes for each column. They can use their memories and textbooks—but no dictionaries.

03 Call time after 15 minutes. Ask each pair to state the number of characters they have written down. The pair that wrote the most, of course, wins.

The class then reviews the characters together. Have volunteers come to the board to write representative characters adding one stroke to their character at a time. For instance, 吗 would take six separate "unfinished characters" until the finished character 吗 was written. Have the class evaluate their stroke order. What did they get right? What did they get wrong?

Sample

含两个笔画的汉字	含三个笔画的汉字	含四个笔画的汉字	含五个笔画的汉字	含六个笔画的汉字	含七个笔画的汉字	含八个笔画的汉字	含九个笔画的汉字
人	大	夫	田	忙	坐	国	是

10 Air-Writing Characters

FOCUS The physical act of writing in the air makes a deep cognitive impression. Not only does air-writing strengthen muscle memory through exaggerated movement, but it also forces students to mentally visualize each successive stroke and hold it in their brains for a substantially longer period of time than if writing with pen and paper. Furthermore, this activity is particularly beneficial for those students who often become distracted critiquing the aesthetics of their own characters.

LEVEL Elementary—Advanced ★ ★ ★   **TIME** 5—15 minutes

PROCEDURE

01 The teacher prepares index cards with one previously studied Chinese character per card. Prepare at least as many cards as there are students.

02 The class is divided into two teams. One student on Team A comes to the front of the classroom, selects a card from the prepared pile of cards, and then, with his or her back to the class, air-writes the character. Both teams then try to guess which character he or she is writing. The first team to call out the correct answer wins a point.

03 Then a player on Team B comes forward, and so forth, until every student has a chance. The team that guesses the most characters wins.

Below are more challenging variations:

About-Face: Students air-write the character facing the class, as a native speaker of Chinese would do.

Student-Selected Characters: Instead of the teacher making the cards, each team makes the cards that the opposing team must write. The piles from both teams are placed face down in the front of the room. Students from Team A select from the pile created by Team B, and vice versa. Note that in this version, only one team can do the guessing at a time since the team that created the cards would have an unfair advantage.

Über Competition: In this challenging version, either compound words or entire sentences are used.

11 Root Search

FOCUS Just as learning Latin improves one's English, understanding the "roots" (or radicals) within characters betters one's Chinese. This activity focuses on building the scaffolding necessary for students to deepen their understanding—and thereby their recall—of Chinese characters.

LEVEL Elementary—Advanced ★ ★ ★

TIME Preliminary Teaching: 10—15 minutes
Homework: N/A
In-Class Activity: 20 minutes

PROCEDURE

— Preliminary Teaching & Homework —

01 In advance, jot down a list of previously studied characters which the students have had difficulty remembering. This list should have as many characters as there are students. Now, make another list of unfamiliar "crazy" characters that have a wide range of component parts. This list, too, should have as many characters as there are students. Put each word on its own index card, being sure to keep the two piles separate.

02 During a lesson after you have broken down a character into its component parts for better understanding, introduce the assignment. In other words, interrupt your own class by abruptly asking the students to select one card from each of the two piles. Explain that for homework they are to use a dictionary and/or on-line etymological tools (such as on yellowbridge.com or chinesecharacter.org) to prepare a presentation explaining how their characters break down into component parts, and the meaning of those parts.

03 There is no need for them to hand in a written version of their presentations. The odds are that they will do a good job. However, be prepared to step in when necessary.

── In-Class Activity ──

01 At some point later on in the course, write each character from the first pile on its own individual sheet of paper. The paper should be as big as possible. Cut up each character into its component parts or groups of component parts. Tape the "parts" in scrambled fashion up on the board.

02 Divide the class in half and have two students from each team race to make a character. Once a student has made a character, their teammate can go to the board, and so forth down the line.

12 Look It Up, Fast!

FOCUS In this age of high-tech tools, paper dictionaries are often misguidedly seen as obsolete by teachers and students alike. An excellent case, however, can be made that they still serve an important role in language acquisition. Why? First, going through the somewhat laborious process of looking up characters and words focuses students' attention. As a result, retention is indeed often greater. Moreover, the students' curiosity is sparked by seeing the character in a variety of contexts and pairings. Even if a word's definition is forgotten over time, the habit of concentrating on the component parts of characters is an invaluable asset for the Chinese language learner and needs to be fostered. Lazily looking things up in an electronic dictionary may be convenient, but in the long run works against the students. In other word, sharp tools make for dull minds.

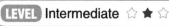 **LEVEL** Intermediate ☆ ★ ☆ **TIME** 20—30 minutes

PROCEDURE

01 In preparation, the teacher creates some words that the students will look up in a Chinese-English dictionary. Choose words that the students have not encountered yet and most likely will not encounter for some time—and that demonstrate how cleverly designed the Chinese language is. Also, be sure to select a mix of characters whose radicals are in varied positions. In other words, some characters' radicals are on the top and bottom, others' are on the left and right, and so on. For instance, 魅力, 秘密, 榴莲, 嗡, etc.

02 Hand out dictionaries to the students. If there is a shortage of dictionaries, one dictionary per pair of students works well. If pressed to find enough Chinese-English dictionaries, the stronger students in the class can use a Chinese-only dictionary either aimed for children or adults.

03 · Pick a model word and tell students, step by step, how one goes about looking up a Chinese word. *(See Sample.)*

04 · Once all students have found the model word in the dictionary, hand out the list of words that need to be looked up and tell them that "the race is on." The first student (or pair of students) who writes the *pinyin* and definition for all items wins. If a student is using a Chinese-only dictionary, he or she can just write down the *pinyin* and the teacher can help with the definition.

NOTE

For students working in pairs, be sure that one student does not hog the dictionary. One student can count the number of strokes, while the other first tries to find the radical and then the word in the dictionary. Then they can switch tasks.

Sample

How to Use a Chinese Dictionary*

When you come across a Chinese character or compound word that you don't recognize and can't guess at its pronunciation, you can look it up by using the radical index.

FIND THE RADICAL: Let's say you want to look up the compound word 确认. The first step is to determine which part of the first character is the radical. In this case, the radical of 确 is 石. Now count the number of strokes of the radical. 石 has 5

14　部首目录

78	见	42	[77]	(水)	42	134	舌	55	159	邑	61	186	音	69
79	牛(牜)	42	105	目	50	135	竹(⺮)	55	160	身	61	187	首	69
80	手	42	106	田	50	136	臼	56	[49]	(足)	31	[63]	(韋)	34
[80]	(产)	44	107	⺲	50	137	自	56	161	釆	61	[57]	(鬼)	33
81	气	44	108	皿	50	138	血	56	162	谷	61		十画	
82	毛	44	[176]	(钅)	65	139	舟	56	163	豸	61	188	髟	69
[74]	(攵)	38	109	生	51	140	色	56	164	龟	62	[58]	(馬)	33
83	长	44	110	矢	51	141	齐	56	165	角	62	189	高	69
84	片	44	111	禾	51	142	衣	57	166	言	62	190	鬥	69
85	斤	44	112	白	51	143	羊	57	167	辛	63	191	鬲	69
86	爪	44	113	瓜	51	[143]	(⺷)	57		八画			十一画	
87	父	45	114	鸟	51	[143]	(⺶)	57	168	青	63	[149]	(麥)	60
[34]	(爿)	25	115	疒	52	144	米	57	169	其	63	[156]	(齒)	60
[86]	(灬)	45	116	立	53	145	聿	58	170	雨(⻗)	63	[177]	(鱼)	67
88	月	45	117	穴	53	[145]	(⺺)	58	171	非	63	192	黄	69
89	氏	46	[142]	(衤)	57	146	艮	58	172	齿	63	193	麻	69
90	欠	46	[145]	(血)	58	147	羽	58	[130]	(虎)	54	194	鹿	69
91	风	46	[118]	(⻖)	53	148	糸	58	173	黾	64		十二画	
92	殳	46	118	疋	53		七画		174	隹	64	195	鼎	69
93	文	46	119	皮	53	149	麦	59	175	阜	64	196	黑	69
94	方	46	120	癶	53	150	走	60	176	金	64	197	黍	69
95	火	46	121	矛	53	151	赤	60	[185]	(飠)	68		十三画	
96	斗	47	[99]	(母)	48	[68]	(車)	37	177	鱼	67	198	鼓	69
[95]	(⺌)	47		六画		152	豆	60	178	隶	67	[173]	(黽)	64
97	户	47	122	耒	53	153	酉	60		九画		199	鼠	69
[100]	(衤)	49	123	老	53	154	辰	60	179	革	68		十四画	
98	心	47	124	耳	53	155	豕	60	[128]	(頁)	54	200	鼻	69
[145]	(衤)	58	125	臣	53	156	卤	60	180	面	68	[141]	(齊)	57
[45]	(㞢)	29	126	⻄(西)	53	[76]	(貝)	39	181	韭	68		十五画	
99	毋	48	127	而	54	[78]	(見)	42	182	骨	68	[172]	(齒)	64
	五画		128	页	54	157	里	60	183	香	68		十六画	
[61]	(玉)	34	129	至	54	[158]	(⻊)	60	184	鬼	68	[103]	(龍)	49
100	示	48	130	虍	54	158	足	60	185	食	68		十七画	
101	甘	49	131	虫	54				[91]	(風)	46	[164]	(龜)	62
102	石	49	132	肉	55							201	龠	69
103	龙	49	133	缶	55									
[67]	(⺊)	37												
104	业	50												

---

* The sample dictionary is *Contemporary Chinese Dictionary* (6th edition) published by the Commercial Press.

29

strokes. Turn to the radical index and locate the 石 radical under the five-stroke section. Next turn to the page number listed, which in our example is page 49. This is where you will find all the characters that have 石 as the radical.

[100]		(裆)	1632	砂	1390	础	196	硝	1081	(碛)	905	礤	822
礻部		裸	482	矾	357	破	1007	(硚)	1019	**十画**		础	276
一至四画		(裀)	594	矿	757	砼	739	硝	446	(碼)	864	(磯)	598
礼	793	禅	141	砀	262	砉	837	码	6	磴	732	礞	889
机	598		1134	码	864	砻	1080	碘	292	磊	786		196
祁	1017	祿	844	岩	1496	砮	958	硅	331	(磴)	1353	礴	642
礽	1097	祺	1401	矞	556	**六至七画**		碑	54		1360	磻	785
社	1147	禖	882		1468	硎	852	碛	1682	磜	1394	磷	1626
祀	1235	福	402	研	1497	硐	1459	碍	982	磔	1649	(砻)	1080
祃	865	禊	1552		1502	硅	490	硼	298	(碜)	1081	磻	117
袄	1409	(禛)	1653	砆	397	硒	456	碜	585	磉	494	(礽)	802
祎	1532	禔	1669	砖	1709	砣	874	碎	1247	磅	41	(磹)	6
祉	1675	褍	289	砑	157	硒	1391	碌	59	磺	973	磹	757
视	1189	(禋)	1532	砘	1492	硕	1227	碣	983	磬	807	礴	117
祈	1019	禄	1414	砚	332	硖	232	碑	278		1034	(磹)	357
祇	1019	(祸)	865	砒	985	硊	1253	碇	309	(碻)	1081	(礴)	785
(祇)	1673	禛	1654	砌	1029	硖	1402	碗	743	磙	948	(礤)	802
祋	331	禋	1720		1049	硜	1045		744	磻	1121	硼	1682
祊	63	褋	1021	砭	1127	硐	314	碌	1342	磉	971	(礤)	976
五画		(禩)	1235	(砏)	935	砲	1353	碌	835	**十一画**		磷	102
祛	1071	禵	1474	泵	64		1360		1360	磬	1064	磲	919
祜	552	禧	1398	砚	1502	(株)	1696		844	(碛)	1029	(磹)	837
祐	1182	檀	258	斫	1719	研	1046	碎	162	磲	726	礤	1217
祐	1583	(襌)	141	砝	76	硪	935	**九画**		磺	573	(礴)	772
祓	400		1134	砍	725	砧	583	碧	73	(磻)	1709	**103**
祖	1739	(榍)	598	砄	392	(砷)	513	碾	1029	礼	129	**龙部**
神	1155	(禮)	793	砄	709	硌	442	碡	1695	(磬)	739	龙	836
祝	1705	(祠)	266	**五画**			858	(碥)	1653	磬	1029	杂	838
祚	1748	(襕)	892	砟	354	硁	1552	碟	303	(磴)	494	袭	1498
祔	410	襃	1085	砍	4	砮	1634	碴	135	(磴)	1478	龚	837
祗	1669	**101**		砟	97	(砮)	1634	碱	137	磴	1072	垄	837
祢	892	**甘部**		砢	731	(砗)	157	碣	635	礓	766	龛	455
祕	894	甘	420	砸	1617	硬	1565	(碥)	1227	(磹)	835	垄	1395
(祕)	72	邯	509	砺	802	(硖)	1402	(碜)	1632	磨	914	龛	724
	894	某	920	砰	981	硭	739	碥	772	磷	919		1649
祠	212	(甚)	147	砧	1653	硝	1429	(碣)	262	**十二画**		**[103]**
六画以上		曾	425	砠	699	(砚)	1502	碾	665	**以上**		**龍部**
祯	1653	**102**		砷	1153	(砰)	162	碣	1361	(磴)	1045	(龍)	836
裕	1402	**石部**		砟	1631	硪	1370	碣	341	(磴)	232	(龑)	838
祧	1291	石	256	砝	1307	破	633	磋	1264		1253	(襲)	1498
祥	1423		1175	砥	282	硫	1081	磅	327	磷	1262	(龔)	837
祷	266	**二至四画**		砭	802	硪	833	磊	760	礤	1641	(龕)	837
(视)	1189	(矴)	309	砰	935	硪	774	磬	392	礅	278	(龕)	724
祸	594	矶	598	(砲)	976	**八画**		磷	289	(磹)	1046	(壟)	837
祺	679	矸	421	砫	1705	(砗)	1020	磴	227	礓	650	(襲)	455
禚	826	矼	426	砣	766	碁	1383	磺	213	礤	971	(襲)	1395
禖	1020	矻	748	砣	1330	硼	1064	磴	1478	(磺)	332	(襲)	1649
				砩	400	硕	1029	磴	79				

FIND THE CHARACTER: Now count the strokes of the rest of the first character, omitting the radical. Aside from the radical, 确 has 7 strokes. Find the character under the appropriate stroke column, and then go to the page number listed, which in this case is page 1081.

雀 què 图❶鸟，体形较小，发声器官较发达，有的叫声很好听，嘴呈圆锥状，翼长。雌雄羽毛的颜色多不相同，雄鸟的颜色常随气候改变。吃植物的果实或种子，也吃昆虫。种类很多，常见的有燕雀，锡嘴雀等。❷（Què）姓。
另见1045页qiāo；1047页qiǎo。
【雀斑】quèbān 图 皮肤病，患者多为女性。症状是面部出现黄褐色或黑褐色的小斑点，不疼不痒。
【雀鹰】quèyīng 图鸟，体形小，羽毛灰褐色，腹部白色，有赤褐色横斑。脚黄色。雌的比雄的稍大。是猛禽，捕食小鸟。通称鹞鹰。
【雀跃】quèyuè 圆高兴得像雀一样跳跃：欢欣～｜～欢呼。

确¹（確、⁕塙、⁕碻）què ❶形符合事实的；真实的：～正｜～证。❷ 圆 的确；实在：～乎～；～有此事。❸ 坚固；坚定：～立｜～信｜～守。

确² què〈书〉（土地）不肥沃：晓～。

【确保】quèbǎo 圆 确实地保持或保证：～交通畅通｜加强田间管理｜～粮食丰收。
【确当】quèdàng 形 正确恰当：适当｜立论～｜措辞十分～。
【确定】quèdìng ❶ 形 明确而肯定：～的答复｜～的胜利。❷ 圆 使确定：了工作之后就土烦｜还没有～候选人名单。
【确乎】quèhū 圆 经过试验，这办法有效｜屋子又宽绰又豁亮，～不坏。
【确立】quèlì 圆稳固地建立或树立：～制度｜～信念。
【确切】quèqiè 形 ❶ 准确；恰当：～不移｜用字～。❷ 确实；消息～的保证。
【确认】quèrèn 圆 明确承认；确定认可（事实、原则等）；参加会议的各国～了这些原则｜这文物的年代尚未经专家～。
【确实】quèshí ❶ 形 真实可靠；～性｜～的消息｜这件事他亲眼看到，说得确确实实。❷ 圆 对客观情况的真实性表示肯定：他最近～有些进步｜这事～不是他干的。
【确守】quèshǒu 圆 坚定地遵守：～合同｜信义。
【确信】quèxìn ❶ 圆 坚定地相信；坚信：我们～这一崇高理想一定能实现。❷（～儿）图 确实的信息；不管事成与否，请尽快给你～儿。
【确凿】quèzáo（旧读 quèzuò）形 非常确实，～不移｜～的事实｜证据～。
【确诊】quèzhěn 圆 确切地诊断：经过检查，为肺炎。

【确证】quèzhèng ❶ 圆 确切地证实：我们可以～他的论断是错误的。❷ 图 确切的证据或证明：在～面前他不得不承认自己的罪行。

阕（闋）què ❶〈书〉终了；乐（yuè）～。❷ 量 a）歌曲或词一首叫一阕，弹琴～一｜填～一词。b）一首词的一段叫一阕：上～｜下～。❸（Què）图姓。

攉 què ❶〈书〉敲击。❷ 见1081页"榷"。

鹊（鵲）què 图 喜鹊。
【鹊巢鸠占】quècháo-jiūzhàn 比喻强占别人的房屋、土地、产业等。
【鹊起】quèqǐ 圆 像喜鹊忽地飞起，形容名声兴起、传扬：声誉～｜文名～。
【鹊桥】quèqiáo 图 民间传说天上的织女七夕渡银河与牛郎相会，喜鹊来搭成桥，叫作鹊桥：～相会（泛指夫妻或情人久别后团聚）｜搭～（比喻为男女撮合婚姻）。

碏 què 用于人名，石碏，春秋时卫国大夫。

阙（闕）què ❶ 图 古代皇宫大门前两边供瞭望的楼，借指帝王的住所：宫～｜伏～（跪在宫门前）。❷ 神庙、陵墓前竖立的石雕。❸（Què）图姓。
另见1080页 quē。

榷¹ què〈书〉专卖：～茶｜～税（专卖业的税）。

榷²（△攉、⁕搉）què 商讨：商～。

qūn （ㄑㄩㄣ）

囷 qūn 古代一种圆形的谷仓。

逡 qūn〈书〉退让；退。
【逡巡】qūnxún〈书〉圆 有所顾虑而徘徊或不敢前进：～不前。

qún （ㄑㄩㄣˊ）

宭 qún〈书〉图 群居；❷ 某种事物荟萃的地方；学～。

裙（⁕帬、⁕裠）qún 图 ❶ 裙子：布～｜短～｜连衣～｜百褶～。❷（～儿）图形状或作用像裙子的东西：围～儿｜墙～儿。

FIND THE WORD: Under the 确 entry on page 1081, you will see all the words that start with 确—including, of course, 确认. It's listed there somewhere, now go and find it!

Chapter 3
Beefing Up Vocabulary

In this chapter, we stress five areas of vocabulary: compound word formation; antonyms; synonyms; idioms, proverbs, and other sayings; and recycling vocabulary. Altogether, ten activities are presented:

13 Character Web

FOCUS To guide students in discovering the logic of Chinese compound word formation is one of the most important responsibilities that a Chinese language teacher has. In addition to helping students expand their vocabulary, an assignment like this both boosts students' curiosity and shows them the connections they need to make in order to become independent learners of the language.

LEVEL Intermediate—Advanced ☆ ★ ★

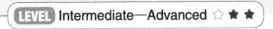

TIME Preparatory Discussion: 20 minutes
Homework Assignment: N/A
Presentation: 5—10 minutes per student

PROCEDURE

01 Discuss with students the characteristics of Chinese that make it a difficult language to learn.

02 Then point out that building vocabulary is relatively easy because of the mnemonic devices built into Chinese characters. Moreover, since such a large percentage of Chinese words are compound words, once you learn one word you are halfway there to learning several others.

03 Give a "character web" demonstration for a compound word *(See Sample.)* preferably one selected from materials that students are currently studying. As you draw your web on the board, ask the students to guess the meanings of the words. This is a great opportunity to both preview and review vocabulary, in full or as component parts of compound words.

04 Assign each student their own compound word for which they are to make their own "vocabulary web." Choose words from present or upcoming course materials that you know will elicit interesting "discoveries" from the students. Also, be sure to stress that this is not an art assignment. Their time should be spent immersed in a dictionary (either a print or online one would be appropriate for this assignment), not on figuring out design software. Pen and paper is just fine.

05 When grading the assignment, circle those words that are useful or particularly interesting, and better yet, ones that will appear in future lessons. Be sure that the selected words link up to one another.

06 Have students present their mini "vocabulary web" to the class, on the board.

NOTE

The sample is a mix of previously studied words and ones which are apt to be of interest.

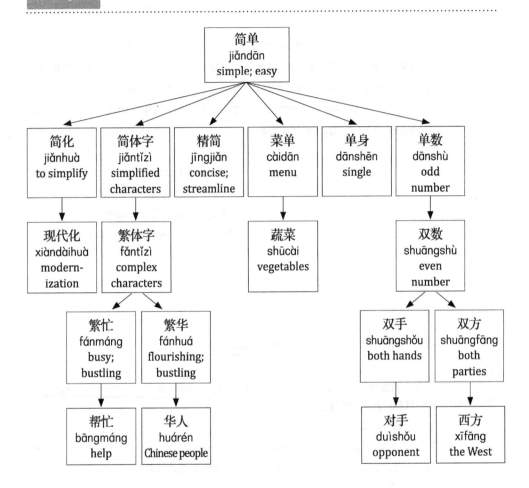

ACTIVITY 14

Compound Word Race

FOCUS This activity is aimed at reviewing vocabulary and further reinforcing students' understanding of the logic of Chinese. By having the students understand the "snowball" nature of vocabulary building, Chinese becomes much less intimidating and students' motivation to study increases.

LEVEL Intermediate—Advanced ☆ ★ ★

TIME Timed Race: 5 minutes
Group Competition: 20 minutes

PROCEDURE

── Timed Race ──

01 Select characters from which compound words can be made. For example:
具: 具体, 家具, 玩具...
解: 解释, 了解, 解决...

For each compound word, prepare two cards, one card with each character on it. The cards with the "base" characters should all be one color, and the cards with the "added" characters should all be a second color. For example, the cards for 具 and 解 should be one color and the cards for 体, 家, 玩, 释, 了 and 决 should be another color. So for this example, there would be a total of 12 cards, half in one color and half in another.

02   Each student or pair of students is given a full, shuffled deck of cards. From the moment the sand clock is turned over or the timer is set, the students see how many cards they can pair up in the given time. If this will be followed with a group competition, the time selected should be such that no students completely finish.

— Group Competition —

To review and consolidate knowledge, it can be helpful to follow with a group competition.

01   Split the class into two (or more, if appropriate) groups. Write the "base" characters on the board with an appropriate number of empty slots beside them. In the above mini-example, 具 would be followed by three blanks. When the teacher says one of the "base" characters, the first team to respond (either by raised hands or call outs) gets to post or write their answer on the board.

02   The rules governing how students put their answer on the board can vary. Students may be asked to say the word and its definition, write down the *pinyin* with appropriate tones, and/or use the word in a simple sentence, perhaps using a set grammar pattern.

No Dilution Here

FOCUS Research clearly shows that learning new words by associating them with previously learned words works, and works well.[*] Thus giving students a list of antonyms is a very effective way to consolidate and boost students' vocabulary—provided they have learned or have been introduced to at least one word from the antonym pair. To further quicken the learning process, one of the best ways to learn antonyms is through the classic game of concentration. The version written in detail below ensures success and maximum participation of all students from the weakest to the strongest. Also included is a quick review option that requires little preparation from the teacher.

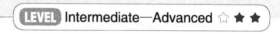
LEVEL Intermediate—Advanced ☆ ★ ★

TIME Concentration: 20 minutes
Ball Toss Review: 5—10 minutes

PROCEDURE

— *Concentration* —

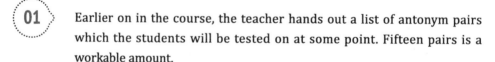

01 Earlier on in the course, the teacher hands out a list of antonym pairs which the students will be tested on at some point. Fifteen pairs is a workable amount.

---

[*] Folse, K.S. *Vocabulary Myths: Applying Second Language Research to Classroom Teaching.* Ann Arbor: The University of Michigan Press, 2004.

02 Some time before the students will be tested, the teacher prepares the materials for the game of concentration. Using letter-sized sheets of paper, held horizontally, the teacher prints one word, in both characters and *pinyin*, as large as possible on each individual sheet. Use the words from the antonym list as well as adding a few that the class has tangentially been introduced to. To avoid transparency, staple a piece of dark colored paper to the back of each sheet. Shuffle the stack to ensure pairs are not in consecutive order. Then number the colored sheets by putting stickers with large Arabic numerals on each one.

03 The teacher tapes all the words in numerical order on the board and/or blank wall. Painter's tape works well on the wall as it is strong enough to hold, yet easy to remove.

04 Ask a student to pick two numbers. (Doing so has the added benefit of reviewing numbers.) The teacher flips the papers to reveal the words and tapes them in their respective positions so that everyone can see, and then flips them back to their original position. When a student uncovers a match, hand the pair to him or her.

05 Most likely the students will call out the revealed words as well as their meanings and/or their antonyms. If they do not, ask them.

06 Students rotate turns until all pairs have been discovered. The student with the most pairs wins.

—— Ball Toss Review ——

01 Choose several antonym pairs that the students have learned previously, and write one word from each pair on the board. Again, fifteen or so is a good amount. Have the students come up with the correct antonym. Write the correct answers on the board as students come up with them. Depending on students' level, characters and/or *pinyin* can be used.

02 Now, erase one word from each of the pairs. Doing so will elicit a collective "uh-oh" from the students.

03 Pair up students of similar ability and give each pair a ball. They are to toss it back and forth while running through the list of antonyms. For example,

- Student A says 懒惰 and tosses the ball to student B.

- Student B catches the ball and says 勤劳.

- Student B then says 干净 and tosses the ball back to student A who will catch it and say 肮脏 and so forth.

04 The first pair of students to finish stating all the antonym pairs on the list wins.

05 You can make this more challenging by adding a particular grammatical structure that the class has recently gone over. For instance, the students might have to say 越来越 before stating the antonyms.

Backs Against the Wall

FOCUS Reviewing vocabulary is paramount in successful language learning—as is practicing the skill of circumlocution. This activity tackles both. Since there are few opportunities for students studying Chinese outside of Chinese-speaking countries to get the satisfaction that comes from effective circumlocution, this activity forces students to communicate on-the-fly—yet in a targeted fashion—thereby simulating real-world pressure.

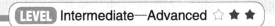 **LEVEL** Intermediate—Advanced ☆ ★ ★   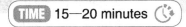 **TIME** 15—20 minutes ⏱

PROCEDURE

01 The class is divided into two teams. Two students, one student from each team, go to the front of the classroom and stand with their backs to the board. They are not allowed to turn around. Selecting from a list of previously studied antonyms, the teacher writes half of an antonym pair on the board. For example, the teacher could write 富有, from the antonym pair 富有 and 贫穷.

02 Teams take turns using Chinese to describe the word on the board. For the above example, they might say: 有钱，可以买很多东西. The two students standing in the front of the class must guess the antonym of the word that their classmates are describing. So in this example, the guessing students would be correct if they say 贫穷. Once one of the students gives the correct answer, the two students sit down and another two come up to guess, and the cycle repeats.

03 Scoring works as follows: A team scores a point if either of the students guesses correctly based on their team's clue. In addition, the student who guesses correctly earns a point for his or her team. So for each word, two points will be allocated. Both points may go to one team or be split between teams depending on which team has given the last successful clue and which team's member has guessed correctly.

NOTE

By design, this is a little tricky. First, the guessing students have to understand their classmates' clues and guess the word being described— and then they must think of that word's antonym. In all likelihood, one of the guessing students will blurt out the word that their classmates are describing, such as 富有 in the above example. This gives their competitor a chance to "steal" by quickly coming up with the antonym 贫穷 which is a much easier task.

I Bet Your Wager

FOCUS Even within the same language, few words share the exact same meaning—and even fewer (if any) can be used interchangeably in all cases. While native speakers gain a sensitivity for word usage through exposure over decades, foreign language learners do not have that luxury. As such, the Chinese language learners need to be expressly taught subtle differences in meaning between synonyms, along with their respective collocations. This activity first has students discover for themselves these differences, and then refines their impressions through a gambling game.

LEVEL Intermediate—Advanced ☆ ★ ★

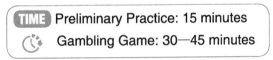

TIME Preliminary Practice: 15 minutes
Gambling Game: 30—45 minutes

PROCEDURE

—— Preliminary Practice ——

01 The teacher prepares a list of synonyms for three to five words that the students have already learned. Ideally, the matching synonyms chosen will appear in future lessons. For example, if the students have already learned 改善, then you can add the synonym 改进. In the case of synonym triplets, if the students have already learned 发现 and 觉察, then 发觉 can be introduced. In total, there should be six to fifteen words (three to five sets of synonyms).

02 Have the students work in pairs or individually. Since synonyms are similar in meaning but not always interchangeable, the students' job is to find out the distinctions between the synonyms. Tell the students they have 15 minutes to do so. They can do this in a variety of ways. One is by looking up the words in a dictionary and noting subtle differences in definitions and/or collocations. If the students have access to the internet, another handy method is for students to use a search inquiry such as 改善和改进的区别. Due to the great number of Chinese language learning sites, the students are bound to find bilingual explanations of the differences.

NOTE

If no students are done in 15 minutes, extend the time—until at least one pair of students is finished. If the students remain focused, by all means let them finish up and leave the next part for another day.

—— Gambling Game ——

01 In advance, the teacher has written three fill-in-the-blank sentences for each pair of synonyms on the board. For example, for the pair 改善 and 改进, the sentences might run along these lines:

a. 工人的生活条件 _____ 了。

b. 你们的工作方法有待 _____。

c. 新校舍建成后，学生的学习环境得到了 _____。

For triplets, three sentences are enough. To "trick" students, one triplet can go unused.

02 Divide the class into two teams. Tell the class that each team has 100 *yuan* to bet. They can wager 5, 10, or 20 *yuan* per blank, depending on how sure they are about their answers. If they guess correctly, they double the amount bet. The team with the most money at the end is, of course, the winner.

03 Team A states how much they are willing to wager on the first blank. Team B then decides whether they want to pass, see the bet, or see the bet and raise it. If Team B wants to pass, then Team A must state their answer. If their answer is correct and they wagered 20 *yuan*, Team A now has an additional 40 *yuan*. If their answer is wrong, 20 *yuan* is subtracted from Team A's total. If Team B wants to see Team A's bet, and does not want to raise it, then a representative from each team writes their respective team's answers on a piece of paper. The teams' totals then are re-calculated based on whether their answers were correct or not. If Team B wants to see Team A's bet and raise it (and Team A doesn't want to match that raise), then Team B must state their answers.

04 After the first blank is filled, the betting begins with Team B, and so forth. After each set of synonyms is completed, spend time discussing why each word is or is not the appropriate fit.

NOTE

In subsequent versions, a nice touch is to add one fill-in-the-blank sentence for a previously studied synonym pair.

ACTIVITY

18 Loaded Words

FOCUS This activity expounds on the previous one by introducing the terms 褒义词, 贬义词 and 中性词. The students undoubtedly will be aware of connotations in their own language and thus will delight in learning the similar subtleties between Chinese words. Not only will students *feel* that they are making progress in the language by covering more sophisticated material, but they in fact will be making progress. Having the ability to ask native speakers about the connotations that particular words carry is an important step in their becoming independent learners of Chinese.

LEVEL Intermediate—Advanced ☆ ★ ★

TIME Classwork: 15-20 minutes
Homework Assignment: N/A
Presentation: 20 minutes

PROCEDURE

— Classwork —

01 In preparation, the teacher thinks of five sets of synonyms that have or will come up in course work and creates a handout in grid format. Place the five sets of synonyms running down a column on the left side of the paper and 褒义词, 贬义词 and 中性词 as separate column headers along the top. Leave enough space for students to write notes. *(See Sample.)*

02 In class, the teacher writes the synonyms scattered in random fashion across the board. Ask for volunteers to come up and circle the pairs with colored chalk. Each synonym pair should be circled in a different color from the others.

爱好　扩张　恳求　后果

扩展　果断　嗜好　结果

乞求　武断

○ 03 ○ Once the pairs have been identified, hand out the grid. Using dictionaries, the students, working individually or in groups, try to determine which words have negative, positive, or neutral connotations. Suggest that students write down a collocation for each synonym. Students who finish early can continue their search online.

○ 04 ○ When the students are done, discuss their findings.

—— Homework & Presentation ——

○ 01 ○ As a homework assignment, have the students write a short essay using just the words with negative connotations.

○ 02 ○ Once the papers are corrected, have the students share their essays with the class.

Sample

	褒义词	贬义词	中性词
结果			
后果			
恳求			
乞求			
扩张			
扩展			
果断			
武断			
嗜好			
爱好			

19 Parallel Proverbs

FOCUS Before students can hope to recognize proverbs in conversation, and not to mention use them themselves, they must over-learn them. This activity supplements the effective necessity of testing by livening things up a bit.

LEVEL Intermediate—Advanced ☆ ★ ★

TIME Preliminary Practice: 10—15 minutes
Extended Practice: 20 minutes

PROCEDURE

—— Preliminary Practice ——

01   In a scattered fashion, the teacher writes previously studied proverbs and idioms in both Chinese and English on the board. Be sure not to unintentionally write the English definition right next to the Chinese one too often. Below is an example:

> 乱七八糟　be prepared for the worst　一口吃不成胖子
> Just deserts.　讨价还价　all sixes and sevens
> 不怕一万，就怕万一
> Rome wasn't built in a day.
> 善有善报，恶有恶报　　haggle

By all means, take this opportunity to throw in a few expressions that have not be studied previously. If doing so, a more literal English version would be a good idea. For example, 画蛇添足 can be translated to "draw a snake and add feet."

02 Divide the class into two teams and give each team a different colored chalk or marker. One student from each team goes to the board. (If the board is large enough to fit four people, two from each team can go up.) If the teacher calls out an expression in Chinese, the students are to circle the English version. If the teacher calls out an expression using English, the students are to circle the Chinese version. The student who first circles the correct version in the "correct" language earns a point for his or her team.

03 Team members rotate until all idioms are circled. The team with the most circled items wins.

—— Extended Practice ——

Since Chinese is chock-full of idioms that have numbers in them, a handy way to cover them is to simply tackle them numerically, one by one. Below is an example set of idioms which begins with the number 一 .

01 In advance, the teacher creates a slideshow of previously selected "numerical" idioms. Using animation, have the characters and *pinyin* appear first, and then the English translations. Afterwards, while going over the literal meaning of the characters within each idiom in class, have the students try to work out what the figurative meaning of the idiom could possibly be, and whether or not there is an English equivalent.

一石二鸟	yìshí-èrniǎo	Kill two birds with one stone.
一字千金	yízì-qiānjīn	Every word is worth its weight in gold.
一五一十	yìwǔ-yìshí	in full detail
一见钟情	yíjiàn-zhōngqíng	fall in love at first sight
一刀两断	yìdāo-liǎngduàn	make a clean break with

一目十行	yímù-shíháng	read quickly
一问三不知	yí wèn sān bù zhī	be entirely ignorant
一寸光阴一寸金	yí cùn guāngyīn yí cùn jīn	Time is money.
一马当先	yìmǎ-dāngxiān	be the first to take the lead

02 After pairing up students of similar aptitude, assign each pair an idiom that matches their proficiency level. Each pair of students are to work together to figure out how to express the meaning of the idiom via actions or pictures. The students are free to consult online references, etc.

03 In the following class, have each pair present their idiom in the fashion of their choosing while the rest of the class guesses which idiom they are modeling.

04 After everyone has done their presentations, conduct a quick review and summary. Also, encourage students to think of some numerical idioms in English, and discuss any noticeable similarities and differences with Chinese idioms.

05 In subsequent classes, the teacher can introduce other numerical idioms such as those containing 二, 三, 四 or 百, 千, 万, etc.

ACTIVITY 20 Proverbial Wisdom Charades

FOCUS Nothing cements the meaning of proverbs and other set phrases in learners' minds better than context. In fact, learning set phrases in isolation as if they were simple vocabulary to be memorized can be problematic as subtle differences and situational appropriateness go unobserved. This activity provides just the sort of memorable context that students need, so as to increase the likelihood of their both recognizing, and perhaps even using, the set phrases in authentic speech and writing.

LEVEL Intermediate—Advanced ☆ ★ ★   **TIME** 20—30 minutes ☽

PROCEDURE

01 The teacher prepares cards containing one previously studied Chinese set phrase per card. Ten cards should be sufficient for most classes.

02 The class is divided into teams of two to four students. After the teams are seated away from each other to ensure secrecy, the teacher passes out one card to each team.

03 The teams spend 15 minutes or so creating skits, using both speech and actions, to illustrate their particular phrase. For example, a team given 莫名其妙 could come up the following*:

Student A：巧克力工厂仍然关着。

Student B：真的吗？我怎么闻到巧克力的香味了？

Student A：*(sniffing)* 我也是，但是你看，门还锁着。

Student B：里面肯定有人。

---

* Skit is based on the well-known children's book, *Charlie and the Chocolate Factory*.

Student A: *(fiddles with imaginary lock)* 不可能，没有人能进去，也没有人能出来。

Students A & B: *(puzzled and shocked)* 真是_____！

After the students have created their skits, each team comes to the front of the classroom and performs their skit. It is the job of the other students to guess what set phrase the team is acting out. The first team to call out the correct proverb wins a point. The team performing is also awarded a point if an opposing team guesses correctly. The team with the most points at the end wins.

NOTE

The teacher should use this opportunity to reinforce the meaning of the set phrases by offering constructive criticism and praise during both the creative and performance stages of the activity.

ACTIVITY
21 Individualized Vocabulary Tests

FOCUS In order to function in a second language, vocabulary is a must. "While without grammar very little can be conveyed, without vocabulary *nothing* can be conveyed" sums up perfectly the importance of learning vocabulary in any language[*]. Learning Chinese vocabulary, however, is even more important—and challenging—because helpful cognates do not exist, as they do in the European languages. This activity customizes vocabulary learning to each student so as to increase students' interest and encourage all students to take an active role in their learning.

LEVEL Elementary—Advanced ★ ★ ★

TIME Quiz Time: 5 minutes per student

PROCEDURE

01 Throughout the school year or semester have students come up with their own list of 50 words that they have always wanted to know how to say in Chinese. The words need not be from their textbooks. In fact, it is best to give students wide latitude in choosing their words, provided, of course, that the words chosen are appropriate for the classroom setting.

For students with poor study habits, it would be wise to instruct students on how best to organize their vocabulary lists. Stress that there should be plenty of space left between entries in order to jot down notes and to make studying easier. The following setup works nicely:

Chinese	*Pinyin*	**English Definition**	**Phrases/Collocation**
参加	cānjiā	join; attend	参加会议；参加工作
新鲜	xīnxiān	new; fresh	很新鲜；不新鲜

---

[*] Wilkins, D. A. *Linguistics in Language Teaching*. London: Edward Arnold, 1972.

Stress that there should be plenty of space left between entries. The more congested their lists, the harder they will be to study from. Collocations are only necessary for words whose usage may not be obvious or may pose problems. Advanced students could add Chinese synonyms and/or antonyms.

02 At a designated time, the teacher collects the students' lists and makes copies so that each student not only has their own list but also those of their fellow classmates.

03 At the end of the marking period or semester, have the students quiz their fellow classmates. This should be for a recorded grade. Testing can take the following forms:

Set Time for Completion: Students take turns sitting in front of the class while their fellow classmates call out the English definition that appears on the student's personalized list. The student's goal is to correctly state all the corresponding Chinese words within five minutes.

Competitive Time for Completion: Same as the above but each student is competing to see whose time is the best. A stopwatch or timer will be necessary.

Über Competition: In this version, the teacher calls out the definitions and all students can respond. The student being tested must beat their fellow classmates in answering. Obviously, the teacher must assess the tenor of the classroom and the individual personalities to decide whether this version would be appropriate. In some cases it could be used just for practice and/or students could have the option of choosing this version for extra credit or a better grade. For further practice, teachers can call out the definitions in Chinese rather than in English.

ACTIVITY 22 — Guess the Homonym

FOCUS This activity is designed to practice the vital skill of circumlocution, while at the same time subtly reinforcing how important studying vocabulary is for effective communication. As Chinese language learners can easily become frustrated with all the different meanings just one single character can have, this activity also reminds them that English too is complicated and has a similar phenomenon to 一字多义.

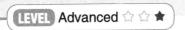 

LEVEL Advanced ☆ ☆ ★   **TIME** 15 minutes

PROCEDURE

01 In preparation, the teacher selects 20 or so English homonyms. For example: *chicken, date, lie, bear, air, book, box, handle, fair, chair, check, current, bank, patient, light, cow, novel, spring, kind, minor*, etc. The teacher then writes each homonym on its own index card.

02 The class is divided into two teams. One individual on Team A is given a homonym card by the teacher. Using Chinese, the student then tries to have his or her teammates guess the English word by giving them the Chinese definition or other such verbal clues. (*See Sample.*) One point is given for the team that comes up with the English word, and one point for each successful definition given in Chinese. If the team guesses the word solely on hearing only one definition, all members (including the clue-giver) can try to come up with the other definition(s).

03 Then a player on Team B gives it a try.

04 The teams take turns and the player on each team who gives the clues rotates as well. If a team is struggling, the other team can "steal" and guess the answers. It is best to leave whether enough time has elapsed and thus "theft" is allowable up to the discretion of the teacher. In addition, if both teams are stumped, the teacher can then start giving clues which are open to either team to answer.

NOTE

The teacher must choose the card since some words are more difficult to describe and thus are more suited for stronger students and vice versa.

Sample

English	Chinese definition	Sample circumlocutions
chicken	鸡； 胆小的	吃的东西，一种动物； 怕这个，怕那个
date	约会； 日期	和女朋友看电影； 1911 年 11 月 10 日
lie	躺下； 说谎	在床上睡觉； 故意讲假话

Chapter 4

Internalizing Grammar I

To aid students in acquiring a good feel for Chinese grammar, we have identified five difficult syntactic elements. They are: measure words, Chinese adverbs, relative clauses, Chinese complements, and expressing "tenses" in Chinese. Two activities were created for each. The activities, ten in total, are as follows:

ACTIVITY 23

First Stop: Measure Words

FOCUS For many Chinese language learners, mastering the abundant variety of Chinese measure words can be a rather confusing and frustrating affair. To smooth out this endeavor, time this activity before the first appearance of measure words in their textbook for maximum reinforcement. Time this activity before the first appearance of measure words in their textbook for maximum reinforcement.

LEVEL Elementary ★ ☆ ☆    **TIME** 20 minutes

PROCEDURE

01 Divide the students into groups of three or four. Ask the students to jot down objects in the classroom and how many there are of each of them. For example, one blackboard, twenty desks, twenty-five chairs, etc. Be sure to deliberately bring in objects that are normally not in the classroom in order to add variety to the measure words needed.

02 The students are then to use an online translator tool to translate their findings into Chinese. Ask the students to discuss the Chinese translations and figure out the differences between English and Chinese. If the site has a speaking option, by all means have the students use it.

03 Once the students get the hang of this, hand out a different colored piece of chalk or a marker to each team. Tell them to continue translating, but also have them write their Chinese translations on the board. The team that is able to write down the most Chinese translations wins.

04 Use your discretion on when to call time. After the winning team is declared (and errors corrected), have a little discussion. Ask the students if they notice anything going on? If they do not, guide them by pointing out the nouns. Since they have already learned numbers, they will now notice the characters in between. Briefly explain the use of measure words in Chinese. Contrast with English which rather infrequently uses "units" when counting or pointing out specific objects.

05 From the board, choose three of the most useful translations and have the students memorize them for a quiz the following period. In all likelihood, they will be some variation of 一本书 , 一杯茶 , 一张纸 . For the quiz, by all means alter the quantities to give the students further practice with their numbers.

ACTIVITY 24 What Did I Just See?

FOCUS This activity is aimed at moving students away from relying on the general classifier 个. It is important to emphasize to students that using the appropriate measure words aids native Chinese speakers in comprehending foreigners' speech, which may be riddled with non-native pronunciation and incorrect tones. Perhaps more importantly, becoming accustomed to measure words aids in their own understanding of native Chinese speakers. Small items can often make a big difference in being both understood and understanding others.

LEVEL Elementary—Intermediate ★ ★ ☆   **TIME** 5—10 minutes

PROCEDURE

01 In preparation, the teacher brings in a variety of objects which require different measure words. For example:

- two photos 两张照片
- one pen 一支钢笔
- one coat 一件外套
- one letter 一封信
- three books 三本书
- one computer 一部电脑

Ten to fifteen items should suffice.

02 One by one, the teacher places the objects on a table in full view of the class and while doing so says what the objects are. Depending upon the level of the students, the teacher can increase the difficulty by adding descriptors to the objects. For example: 三本关于历史的书, 一支红色的笔, etc.

03 The students are given a few minutes to remember all the objects. Then

60

they are divided into teams. The teacher now covers the table with a piece of cloth to hide the objects.

The first member on Team A says: 我看到+(数词)+(量词)+(物品). Then the first member on Team B does likewise, but his stated item cannot be the same one as his opponent. If he does repeat an item, he forfeits his team's turn. This ensures that the students are listening to their classmates. Teams rotate until all the items have been stated. The team that has remembered and correctly stated the most items with their corresponding numbers and measure words wins.

NOTE

Some students may take note of the fact that there is something else on the table: a piece of cloth. This can be used to decide a tie. The teacher can also sit on the table to break a tie as well.

Happening Adverbs

FOCUS Imagine a world without adverbs. How would we describe how something happened, when something happened, where something happened, or why something happened? Stories would just be a string of bland statements. What better way for students to practice the placement and use of adverbs than storytelling. This activity leads beginning students to tell stories chock full of those indispensable adverbs.

LEVEL Elementary ★ ☆ ☆   **TIME** 10—20 minutes ⏱

PROCEDURE

01 First, select previously studied adverbs that could use some review. A good beginning set might be: 也 , 都 , 只 , 就 and 还 .

02 Propose to the class a "happening" to which the students as a class will tell a story using the previously selected adverbs. Write the "happening" and the required adverbs on the board. For instance, let's say that the "happening" is "在饭馆吃饭的时候，你们发现钱不够了" and you want them to use the above five adverbs. Below is a sample of a class's story aided by the teacher asking leading questions.

Teacher: 你们在哪儿?

Student: 我们都在饭馆吃饭。

Teacher: 小王 (*pick a student's name*) 也在吗?

Student: 他也在。

Teacher: 你们吃了什么?

Student: 我们吃了鸡。

Teacher: 还有呢？

Student: 我们还吃了肉和鱼。

Teacher: 很多东西！很贵，是不是？

Student: 是。

Teacher: 服务员 (waiter) 说了什么？

Student: 他要钱。

Teacher: 他要多少钱？

Student: 五百块。

Teacher: 你们有吗？

Student: 我们只有一块。

Teacher: 他还要多少？

Student: 他还要四百九十九块。

Teacher: 那你们怎么办呢？

Student: 我们就帮他洗碗吧。

Since your students have just begun studying Chinese, keep it as simple as possible. If you need to use a word they have not studied yet, briefly state it in their native tongue, write it on the board, and move on.

03 After they have successfully completed one "happening," select another. This time be sure to aid and encourage the more hesitant students to contribute a line if they had not done so previously.

04 A quiz in the next class asking the students to write down the story is nice reinforcement.

26 Plug-in Adverbs

FOCUS That Chinese words often can be used as more than one part of speech presents a particular difficulty for Chinese language learners. A point often overlooked is that Chinese parts of speech do not directly correlate to the way in which parts of speech are understood or used in European languages. While the value of adding parts of speech to Chinese-English dictionaries is a question for another day, there is one part of speech that is worth drawing students' attention towards: the adverb. Knowing which words function as adverbs and where they should be placed is a grammatical explanation that indeed clarifies rather than complicates.

LEVEL Elementary—Advanced ★ ★ ★   **TIME** 20 minutes

PROCEDURE

01 Prior to the start of class, the teacher writes a short story on the board that does not contain adverbs. Be sure that the story recycles previously studied vocabulary and sentence structures.

02 Ask the students to call out Chinese adverbs that they know. The class can either focus on recently studied adverbs or on a particular category of adverb, for example, adverbs expressing time (已经, 将要, 正在); frequency (总是, 很少, 常常); scope (都, 一起, 只); degree (很, 挺, 比较); or manner (猛然, 连忙, 悄悄). As students call out adverbs, the teacher should write them on the board. For useful ones that the students have studied but cannot recall, the teacher can pantomime to jog students' memories.

03 Then the teacher very slowly begins to read the story. The students are to call out 副词 (or "adverb" in English to drive the point home) when they think that an adverb can be inserted. Once the students call out, the teacher stops reading and takes suggestions on which adverb would be appropriate. The teacher then inserts a star where the adverb goes and repeats the phrase with the suggested adverb included.

04 The student whose adverb suggestion was selected slowly reads the story from the beginning while inserting the chosen adverb where the star is placed. As the student continues reading, the other students once again are to call out 副词 when they think that an adverb can be inserted and then give a suggestion on which adverb would be appropriate. The teacher then inserts a star where the adverb goes and repeats the phrase with the suggested adverb included.

05 The cycle is repeated with the winner being the last person who reads the entire story with all adverbs included.

27 Relative Clause Shuffle

FOCUS Since relative clauses in English are nearly always placed after the noun they modify and are usually introduced using relative pronouns, the Chinese tendency to pile all different types of attributives before the noun they modify can really hamper students' comprehension. An activity which focuses on the general order in which attributives appear provides students with one of the central keys to unlocking the meaning of Chinese sentences.

LEVEL Intermediate—Advanced ☆ ★ ★   **TIME** 10—15 minutes ⏱

PROCEDURE

01 The teacher writes down two or more relative clause phrases with each of the different types of attributives and the final noun placed on a different colored piece of paper. For example:

(purple)	(green)	(yellow)	(pink)	(red)	(white)
possessive attributive	demonstrative+ (numeral)+ measure word	verbal attributive	adjectival attributive	nominal attributive	NOUN
我的	那两位	刚从美国来的	年轻的	巴西	同事
妈妈的	这件	朋友送给她的	红色的	羊毛	围巾

02 Either using tape or magnets, the teacher affixes the final noun of the first phrase at the far right of the board, and then tacks up the attached attributives in a random order.

03 Divide the students into two teams. Working on the first phrase that the teacher has tacked up in a random order, the teams rotate by having one of their teammates state the proper placement of one attributive. (Depending on the layout of the classroom having students physically move the attributives is an option as well.) The teams take turns, with a different teammate placing an attributive each time, until the phrases are in the proper order. The first team that makes the final move and declares that the phrase is indeed in the correct order wins.

04 Looking at the phrases in the correct order, the teacher goes over the general order of attributives. The teacher then tacks up the second phrase and the students have another competition which will undoubtedly be at a much quicker pace.

ACTIVITY 28

Guess the Relative Clause

FOCUS As relative clauses are handled so differently in Chinese and English, students often find them especially challenging to work with. This activity further consolidates students' grasp of Chinese relative clauses by requiring students to rely on their verbal memory, but in a repetitive fashion, which will smooth the transition into making Chinese relative clauses second nature. "Guess the Relative Clause" is particularly helpful after "Relative Clause Shuffle" and/or formal instruction.

LEVEL Intermediate—Advanced ☆ ★ ★   **TIME** 10—15 minutes

PROCEDURE

01 The teacher prepares in advance a relative clause phrase that contains different types of attributives. Using 我的两本刚买的有用的汉语词典 as an example, the teacher then writes down the following on the board:

(purple)	(green)	(yellow)	(pink)	(red)	(white)
possessive attributive	demon-strative+ (numeral)+ measure word	verbal attributive	adjectival attributive	nominal attributive	NOUN
					词典

In other words, only the final noun is known. The rest of the clause is a mystery for the students to deduce. If the class has already done the "Relative Clause Shuffle," the attributive titles ideally should be written in the same color as the colored paper that they appeared upon before.

68

02 Divide the students into two teams. Students take turns guessing the nominal attributive. For example, in the above example, students might say 汉语词典. However, if and when they don't guess correctly, the teacher then starts giving hints.

03 Once the correct answer has been guessed, students must guess the adjectival attributive. Once a team guesses that correctly, everyone moves on to guess the next attributive that appears directly to the left, and so on. However, each guess made must state all previous attributives in the correct order.

04 The first team that is able to say the complete phrase correctly wins. A tie can be broken by having teams make sentences that contain the phrase. To liven up the atmosphere, and this is particularly the case in large classes with students of disparate abilities, it is best just to allow teams to call out answers. The teacher can then use discretion on when it would be appropriate to single a student out to answer.

Consequential Complements

FOCUS In far too many introductory Chinese textbooks, verbs are predominately taught as isolated words—and not in the form that Chinese verbs most often appear, that is, followed by complements. As a result (no pun intended), when students move on with their studies and encounter more authentic Chinese, they need a period of time to accustom themselves to verbal complements. The following two options cover the first Chinese complements that students are likely to encounter in their textbooks (the descriptive), and then the one that they are most likely to stumble across in real life (the resultative).

LEVEL Elementary—Advanced ★ ★ ★

TIME 10—15 minutes for descriptive complement
20—30 minutes for resultative complement

PROCEDURE

— Descriptive Complement —

• DESCRIBE TO ME

01 Have students individually select five action verbs or phrases that they have learned.

02 Pair up the students. Using the action verbs or phrases that they have previously selected, they are to ask each other questions using the following as a model.

Student A: 你喜欢打篮球吗?

Student B: 我很喜欢打篮球。/ 我不喜欢打篮球。

Student A: 你（**打**）篮球打得好吗 ?/ 你（**打**）篮球打得怎么样?

Student B: 我（**打**）篮球打得很好。/ 我（**打**）篮球打得不好。

03 For homework, the students are to interview a Chinese language learner or a native Chinese speaker about their experience doing something, using their five verbs or phrases. If possible, have the students videotape their interviews using a smart phone or digital camera. If the class has an online discussion board, the students can upload their videos there.

04 After the students have created their videos (or handed in their interviews), meet with each student to go over their work being sure to highlight the good and the not-so-good.

• CHARADES VERSION

In preparation, create separate slips of paper with various actions along with descriptive complements written on them. For instance, 吃饭吃得很慢, 唱歌唱得不好, etc. Hand out two slips of paper to each student and then divide the class into teams. Teams and players then take turns acting out their phrases while the other teams compete to be the first to describe what the person is doing using the correct phrase.

—— Resultative Complement ——

• THE SEARCH FOR COMPLEMENTS

This review activity will take students away from stale textbook text and let them discover real-world examples of Chinese verbal complements in action.

01 The teacher first conducts a little review by asking students why Chinese verbs are often followed by complements of result. If the students are still unsure as to why, make up a sentence such as 他吃午饭了, and then ask the students whether he is full or not. Explain how in Chinese tacking on 可是没吃饱 to the sentence does not defy logic since Chinese action verbs by themselves do not indicate the conclusion nor the result of the particular act. A less extreme example is 买 denoting shopping rather than buying.

02 Then ask the students to recall pairs of action verbs or phrases and their resultative complements. As the students call out their answers, write them on the board. For example:

> 说错　　看到　　听见　　做完　　学会
>
> 记住　　听懂　　做错　　买到　　吃饱　　看懂

03 Each student selects two "verb-complement compounds" to look up on the internet. For example, if a student is looking up 看到, they type 看到 (with the quotations) into the news section of an internet search engine. Their job is to find a sentence that is both interesting and within their comprehension grasp. As the students are working on this, be sure to point out the large number of search results, which will show the students just how important these verbal complements are in Chinese.

04 Each student then selects one of their "pairs" to present to the class. This is a great opportunity to add interesting real-life collocations (as opposed to boring textbook examples) to their repertoire.

• ALTERNATIVE

If you find that your students are addicted to their smart phones and the like, by all means alter the activity. Instead of searching on the internet for specific verb-complement compounds, have students pick out five or more sentences that contain verb-complement compounds from magazines, newspapers and/or clippings that you provide. This more challenging version requires more skimming on the part of the students and thus is ideally suited for advanced students.

What Goes Up Must Come Down

FOCUS Directional complements are the bêtes noires of Chinese language learners. For those who are studying in a non-Chinese locale, their difficulty is even more pronounced. Directional complements are a prime example of success in the classroom often not transferring to success outside the classroom. Facility with their use takes time and significant real-life exposure. Through using memorable scenarios, this activity simulates "outside" success.

LEVEL Intermediate—Advanced ☆ ★ ★

TIME Classwork: 20 minutes
Presentation: 5 minutes per group

PROCEDURE

01 The teacher thinks of scenarios from which students can write a short cartoon strip using four related directional complements. Providing scenarios for the students is important here. Without doing so, the students will waste time thinking in their native tongue, rather than successfully using Chinese—which is, of course, our goal.

02 Once the scenarios are created, print them out along with the required directional complements to be used on half sheets of paper. (*See Sample A—D.*).

03 Divide the students into pairs and explain the assignment while handing each pair their designated scenario. If necessary, give a mini example, such as the following "answer" to the first scenario:

哥哥站在楼上对正在楼下玩游戏的弟弟发命令："快点，把吸尘器搬上来，吸完尘后再把吸尘器搬下去。"弟弟一边玩游戏一边冲着哥哥喊："你先把吸尘器<u>搬上去</u>，然后告诉我，我再来吸，吸完尘，你把吸尘器<u>搬下来</u>。"哥哥说："那算了，我洗衣服吧。快把你的脏衣服放到洗衣机里！"弟弟说："好，等一下。"十分钟后，哥哥走进洗衣房，大声问弟弟："要洗的衣服都<u>放进去</u>了吧？"没有回音，哥哥打开洗衣机，只见里面空空的，气愤地喊着："你为什么没有把衣服<u>放进来</u>？"

04 Obviously, pairs will work at different speeds. The more advanced students can work on improving their basic cartoon while the others are still working on the basic structures. When all the pairs have reached a satisfactory stopping point, collect their work.

05 After you have corrected their work, hand it back and explain that each pair will "draw" and write their cartoon before the class. A good idea is to stagger the students' performances by having only one or two pairs present a day, thereby extending the students' exposure to directional complements.

Sample A

Directional Complements To Be Used: 搬＋上来、搬＋上去、搬＋下来、搬＋下去

"Aghh! My sons are such lazy bones!," grumbles their mother. For the first time in their lives, she decides to give them some chores to do. She starts out small so as not to shock their systems. They are to carry the vacuum upstairs and the laundry downstairs. The fighting between the two brothers ensues....

Sample B

Directional Complements To Be Used: 走＋进来、走＋进去、走＋出来、走＋出去

A couple goes jogging together on their first date. As evening approaches, they decide to extend their date by going dancing. But first they need to stop by the girl's apartment so she can change clothes. When they get to her apartment, she goes into the bedroom to change and closes the door behind her. Half an hour later, her date is getting antsy and asks her to hurry up. After another half an hour goes by, he starts to open the door....

Sample C

Directional Complements To Be Used: 冲＋进来、冲＋进去、冲＋出来、冲＋出去

Three siblings, two sisters and one younger brother, once again have overslept. It is 7:00 a.m. Their school bus comes to pick them up at 7:20 a.m. Upon awakening, the younger sister makes a mad dash to the bathroom leaving her two siblings locked outside the door. The clock ticks....

Sample D

Directional Complements To Be Used: 开＋回来、开＋回去、开＋过来、开＋过去

Two policemen are training their new puppy. Brimming with confidence in their dog training abilities, they let the puppy off lead while in a park near the police station. In a matter of seconds, the puppy is bounding across the nearby interstate....

31 Back to the Future

FOCUS After students have learned and practiced, through classic drills and exercises, the various aspect markers, adverbials, and temporal indicators which Chinese uses to express what in English is conveyed by verbal tenses, the time comes to bring it all together. The flexible nature of this activity allows it to be customized not only to the students' current ability, but also to nicely dovetail it to course content by thoughtful selection of the picture used in the activity.

LEVEL Intermediate—Advanced ☆ ★ ★

TIME Review: 5—10 minutes
Activity: 10—20 minutes

PROCEDURE

01 First, conduct a review of Chinese "tense" indicators. Write "Past," "Completed," "Present," "Continuing," and "Future" on the board.[*] Ask students how does Chinese indicate these states of being. Under the appropriate heading write down, and supplement when necessary, the students' answers. For instance, results may look something like this:

	Past	Completed	Present	Continuing	Future
AFFIRMATIVE	动词＋过	动词＋了	正／在／正在＋动词＋（呢）	动词＋着	要／快＋动词＋了
NEGATIVE	没＋动词＋过	没＋动词	没（＋在）＋动词	没＋动词＋着	还没＋动词＋呢

02 Display a compelling picture of something about to happen. For example: a menacing nurse preparing to give someone a shot; an angry boss facing his employees, etc. Just make sure that the students already know the

---

* The above five states and accompanying structures were extracted from 李德津，程美珍．外国人实用汉语语法．北京：华语教学出版社，1988.

vocabulary necessary to comfortably comment on the picture you select. Anticipate what their possible responses will be and if there is a word or two that might be helpful, write that down on the board. However, try to keep that to a minimum in order to keep the focus on the task at hand, which is expressing time in Chinese.

03 Ask the students questions to prompt them to use the various aspect markers, adverbials, and temporal indicators. Of course, the questions will depend on both the picture and the students' responses, but the following is a good start:

- 你们看到了什么？ (to elicit use of "present" time markers)

- 你们觉得接下来会发生什么事？ (to elicit use of "future" time markers)

- 为什么……? (to elicit use of "past" time markers)

NOTE

Often times, students want to express themselves as they would in their native tongues. Remind them that success in a foreign language is getting your point across—not flawless native language fluency. Instead, encourage your students to use what they already know. For instance, if a picture shows a teacher yelling at his or her students, your students might want to use native-language equivalents of words such as 听话, 淘气, 作弊, 考卷, etc. that they have not studied yet. Nudge them to use the simplified equivalents 不听老师的话 or 看别人的考卷 by asking questions such as 老师说的话，学生都听了吗？ Or 考试的时候，学生们只看自己的考卷吗？ Then, if appropriate, introduce them to other ways to express the same idea.

Instead of a picture, a short three-to-five-minute scene from a movie or television serial can be used.

ACTIVITY

32 — What Goes Before What?

FOCUS When students find that Chinese verbs do not undergo conjugation to express tense, they invariably breathe a sigh of relief. Yet, after that feeling of relief there often comes a sense that "It can't be that easy, can it? I must be missing something." Well, in a way it is that easy. Recent research supports many Chinese language teachers' impressions that Chinese language learners are remarkably accurate in interpreting Chinese temporal indicators.[*]

Yet, for Chinese language students, that lingering doubt remains—even at the advanced level. As such, this activity is designed to lift the "time fog" by showing students exactly how the Chinese language indicates time without morphological tenses—and exactly how successful they themselves are at deciphering Chinese temporal clues.

 Intermediate—Advanced ☆ ★ ★   20—30 minutes

PROCEDURE

01 The teacher prepares a short story of approximately ten sentences in length. The story need not be original, but should have a variety of aspect markers, adverbials, and other temporal clues so that the students will be successful in determining the appropriate order of the sentences. *(See Sample.)*

02 The teacher then prepares an envelope for each student or pair of students which contains the story's ten (or however many) sentences— each written separately on strips of paper. Care should be given to make

---

* Slabakova, R. Acquiring Temporal Meanings Without Tense Morphology: The Case of L2 Mandarin Chinese. *The Modern Language Journal*, 2015(2).

sure that the strips of paper are shuffled before putting them in the envelopes, otherwise you will be doing the students' work for them.

03 The students' job is to put the sentences in the appropriate order for the story to make sense. Once the students are done, have the class see which team came closest to the story's actual order.

04 Together as a class, analyze the story sentence-by-sentence by asking the students why they chose to put each sentence in a particular spot. What clues did they use?

NOTE

A quick comparison to the students' native tongue by highlighting the various tenses required to tell the story in their own language can be illustrative.

Sample

1. 那是一个漆黑的、下着暴雨的夜晚。

   It was a dark and stormy night.

2. 十一点了，街上什么人都没有，只有她自己。

   It was 11 o'clock and the streets were empty—all except for her.

3. 今天她太忙了，晚饭还没吃，完全忘了时间。

   It had been such a busy day that she had totally lost track of all time and hadn't even eaten dinner.

4. 她自言自语道："我得赶紧回家吃饭。"

   She said to herself, "I really should be getting home to eat."

5. 突然，她听到厚底鞋的声音。

   Suddenly she heard the sound of platform shoes.

6.　她走得慢了一点儿，脚步也慢了下来。

She slowed her pace; and the footsteps slowed down too.

7.　她停下脚步，看看周围，却没有发现任何人。

She stopped to look around. There was no one.

8.　她接着赶路，并告诉自己："没有什么可怕的。"

She started up again all the while telling herself, "I will not be scared."

9.　她加快了脚步，但那些脚步也走得更快了。

She quickened her pace, but the footsteps quickened too.

10.　最后，她飞快地跑了起来，跑得那么快，一下子撞上了自己家的前门。

She started to run like crazy. She ran so fast that she crashed into her front door.

11.　这时她低头看着自己的脚，看到了一双厚底鞋。

She then glanced down at her own two feet—and saw a pair of platform shoes.

Chapter 5
Internalizing Grammar II

In this chapter, we continue to focus on Chinese grammar. The concepts in this chapter include questions, existential sentences, serial verbs and complex sentences, the Bǎ Structure, the Bèi Structure, topic-comment, and subject-omitted sentences. Based on these features, we have prepared 14 activities:

ACTIVITY 33

Interrogative Prerogative

FOCUS Chinese is undoubtedly one of the world's hardest languages to learn, which is all the more reason to take advantage of the few simplicities the language does possess. Take the asking and answering of questions. Forming questions in Chinese is just a matter of plugging in question words in the same space that the "answer" would appear in a declarative sentence. Pure simplicity. Yet, students who are accustomed to forming questions via inversion often seem determined to make the simple complex. Do your best to stop them. To help students make that simplicity second-nature, practice is a must for most students. There are a few variations of this activity. The first is a very basic, structured exercise which is appropriate after question-forming has been introduced or as a quick review for struggling students. The "Guess Who" and free-form options are less mechanical in nature and more appropriate when the training wheels are ready to come off.

LEVEL Elementary—Intermediate ★ ★ ☆

TIME 15—20 minutes per activity ⏱

PROCEDURE

—— Structured Basic Version ——

01   To prepare, the teacher creates sets of interrogative "cards" for the students. Using letter-sized paper, held horizontally, the teacher prints out one question word per sheet in both large characters and *pinyin*. A basic set might include 谁, 什么, 哪儿, 怎么样, etc. There should be one set for each student.

02   The teacher writes previously prepared sentences on the board using different colors for each word or words that can be replaced with an interrogative. For example:

(blue)	(red)	(green)
厨师（chúshī）	在厨房（zài chúfáng）	做饭（zuòfàn）。

As a class, go over the sentences to make sure all is understood. For the quicker students, a nice touch is to sprinkle some of the sentences with some vocabulary that they might find interesting.

03 Divide the class into two teams and then hand each student a set of interrogative cards.

04 The teacher then converts the first sentence into a question using the students' native tongue, such as "Where does the chef cook food?" for the above example. When using the students' native language, Chinglish or other language hybrid is strongly recommended. Asking "Chef at where makes food?" reinforces sentence structure and avoids students using precious brain energy to jigger around with unnecessary translations. Keep the sentence simple. Another option is to simply point to the colored word(s), such as 厨师 (chúshī), that you want to be replaced with an interrogative.

05 After the teacher has asked a question, each student then must raise the appropriate card. In this case, it would be 哪儿. The first team to have a majority of its members doing so wins the privilege of having one of its members selected by the teacher to state the question in Chinese. If the student is correct and, for instance, for the above example asks, 厨师在哪儿做饭？, the team wins a point. If not, the opposing team can give it a try.

06 The teacher then forms another question using the same sentence or the next sentence, and so forth.

—— Guess Who? ——

01 In advance, the teacher prepares two sets (Set A and Set B) of four different portrait photographs. Each set should contain photos of world-renowned figures, such as movie stars, athletes, etc. For levity's sake, include some photos of the students in the class and maybe one of the teacher as well. Make as many sets as there are students. Half the class will receive Set A, and the other half will receive Set B.

02 Working in pairs, Student A is given Set A and Student B is given Set B. Student A will begin by secretly looking at the first photo and then asking Student B, "猜猜他/她是谁？" Student B then asks questions that will aid in figuring out who the person is. For instance, "他/她是哪国人？" "他/她是美国人吗？" "他/她做什么工作？" "他/她是老师吗？" "他/她是男的还是女的？", etc. Student A must answer the questions based on facts and can only use English when describing the profession if it is a word that has not be covered yet.

03 If Student B cannot figure out who the person is at this point, asking "他 / 她叫什么名字？" can be used as a last resort. Student A can now say who the person is or simply show the picture to Student B.

04 Student A then selects the second picture, and Student B continues to guess. When all the pictures in Student A's set are used, it is Student B's turn to answer questions and Student A's turn to guess.

—— Free-Form Version ——

01 In preparation, the teacher selects a picture of a prominent, and ideally controversial, world figure.

02 Give the students five minutes or so to write down as many questions that they can which could be directed at this person. The questions need not be all reality-based. In fact, silly ones can give the class a good chuckle. Depending upon the students' level, the teacher might want to provide patterns for them, such as:

Pattern 1: Subject + Verb + Interrogative (+ Object)?

Pattern 2: Interrogative + Verb (+ Object)?

If the students are stuck due to vocabulary, the teacher can give guidance or they can consult an online dictionary.

03 When the time is up, students then present their questions orally to the class while the teacher writes down the questions on the board and makes—or leads the students in making—appropriate corrections.

04 Now have the class select one student to play the role of the famous (or perhaps infamous) figure and one student to act as the "press secretary." The rest of the class will act as reporters at a press conference in which English is not allowed. Each student can only raise one question, which the student posing as the well-known figure and/or the "press secretary" must answer. If they are having difficulty in answering, the teacher can step in as an additional "press secretary." Encourage the stronger students to ad-lib and follow up on an answer given to a previous student's question.

NOTE

Be sure to remind the "reporters" to use polite forms of address and expressions, such as "you" in the polite form, "Mr. President," "May I...," etc.

ACTIVITY 34 — Query Challenges

FOCUS In class and often outside of class as well, language learners spend significantly more time practicing answering questions than asking them. Once the students have the patterns of question-making down, the following gives them concentrated practice in forming relevant questions in a timely manner.

LEVEL Intermediate—Advanced ☆ ★ ★

TIME 10—20 minutes per activity

PROCEDURE

— Excuse Me, May I Ask?* —

01 In preparation, the teacher prepares a short story or joke to tell the class.

02 On the board, the teacher writes question words appropriate for the students' level. For instance, low-intermediate students might see 谁, 哪儿, etc. in *pinyin* and/or characters, whereas advanced students might see 何人, 何处, etc. in characters. The teacher might also wish to add interrogative sentence structure models, "A 还是 B？" "……对不对？" "……（了）没有？".

03 Before beginning the story, tell the students that their objective is to prevent the teacher from finishing the story or reaching the joke's punch line. They do this by interrupting the teacher with questions related to the story. (The question words on the board are simply there to remind the students of the possibilities.) If the questions are constructed correctly, the teacher must answer them before moving on. For example:

---

* This activity has been adapted from Ur, P. *Grammar Practice Activities: A Practical Guide for Teachers*, Cambridge: Cambridge University Press, 2009.

Teacher: 有两个人……

Student: 请问，他们是不是朋友？

Teacher: 是的，他们是朋友。

Teacher: 有两个人在树林中……

Student: 树林在哪个国家？

Teacher: 在德国。

Teacher: 他们很着急地赶路……

Student: 他们为什么很着急？

Teacher: 不太清楚，有可能因为天快黑了。他们很着急地赶路，突然从树林里跑出……

Since many of the questions the students will ask won't have a "true" answer, the teacher can simply make up answers as the story goes on. A good add-on practice is to require that students interrupt you politely by using previously learned vocabulary, such as 请问 , 打扰一下 , 对不起 , 打断一下 , etc.

04 Based on time constraints and how successful the students are, the teacher can decide when and if to tell the remainder of the story.

── What's the Question? ──

Without a doubt if true communication and understanding is our goal, language and cultural literacy cannot be separated. Thus, valuable time should be taken in class to briefly introduce key events and characters in Chinese history. Not only does doing so help in furthering students along the road of cultural literacy, but by having students use Chinese to learn something other than Chinese, students also gain an immensely satisfying sense of achievement. "What's the Question?" is a version of 20 Questions, but with a catch. This activity, where students must ask questions to narrow down on the answer, reviews recently learned knowledge and provides further practice in targeted question creation.

01 After one or more "content" lessons, the teacher makes up cards containing the covered key places, figures, and events that will serve as answers. How many cards is determined by the amount of content covered. At least five should be sufficient.

02 Divide the class into two teams. One student from Team A goes to the front of the room and looks at the first card. Alternating sides, students from each team ask the person questions which can only be answered with a straight "yes" or "no". When ambiguous situations arise, a "hard to say" answer may be necessary. *(See Sample.)*

03 The first team to guess the answer wins that round. Now a student from Team B becomes the answerer, and so forth. The teacher can use their discretion to determine the length of the activity.

NOTE

In classes of varying ability, it is best if the stronger students are selected by the teacher to be the "answerer," or for the teacher to be prepared to interfere and guide weaker students who have the role.

Sample

Student A from Team A: 这是一个人吗?

Student from Team A: 是。

Student A from Team B: 这个人是不是中国人?

Student from Team A: 是。

Student B from Team A: 这个人还活着吗?

Student from Team A: 没有。

Student B from Team B: 这个人修了长城吗？

Student from Team A: 很难说。

Student C from Team A: 这个人是不是秦始皇？

Student from Team A: 是！

ACTIVITY 35

Setting the Scene

FOCUS Telling stories is a great way to learn foreign languages. But to do so effectively, an ability to describe a scene is key. All students, regardless of level, can use extra practice in expressing and describing their observations.

LEVEL Elementary—Advanced ★ ★ ★

TIME 20 minutes per activity

PROCEDURE

—— Elementary Version ——

01 Hand out a drawing of a street scene, such as the picture below. Be sure that the students know the vocabulary necessary to comment on what they see. Anticipate any unknown vocabulary and write it on the board.

02 Divide the students into pairs of more or less equal ability. Tell the students that they will be describing the scene in a series of steps. Write the steps and patterns on the board for guidance. At this elementary stage, don't confuse the students by introducing more precise measure words like 家 unless some of the more advanced students can digest it.

Pattern 1: Simply state what is in the picture by using 有. For example:

有一个花店。

有两个孩子。

Pattern 2: State an object's existence in relation to something else. For example:

花店的左边有一个饭馆。

星巴克的后面有一个公园。

Pattern 3: Increase the complexity by having the students use 着. For example:

花店的对面有几个人站着聊天。

男人的旁边有一个女人遛着鸟。

03 The students should aim for ten sentences for each of the three steps. Pairing students of similar ability makes it easier to help the students. Doing so will also enable you to introduce points, such as the distinction between using 有 and 是, to the more advanced students without making the other students' heads spin.

—— Intermediate-Advanced Version ——

This version serves as a nice warm-up for the "Where in the World?" activity.

01 Take a picture of a local scene which contains people. For maximum interest, the location should be one that students are personally very familiar with. Using a meaningful photograph for the students is much better than bland drawings. Since the photo is just for your personal classroom purposes, there is no concern about copyrights, model releases, etc.

02 Pose a challenge for the whole class: Can everyone describe a part of the scene—but without repeating previously stated descriptions?

03 If towards the end some students cannot come up with anything without restating descriptions from students who have gone previously, note down how many students were able to state novel descriptions. See if the class can top that number later on in the quarter or semester. If, however, they were able to on their first try, the next time around, choose a more challenging photo.

04 Another option is for the students to take photos and challenge their classmates.

NOTE

This can be done with the class divided into two teams or as challenges between smaller groups of students.

ACTIVITY 36 — Where in the World?

FOCUS Existential sentences in and of themselves do not pose a particular challenge for Chinese language learners. With periodic classroom exercises, students usually do not have too much trouble grasping the usages of 是, 有 and V-着. However, putting them together is another matter. This activity serves to consolidate students' prior language knowledge with a motivating expository writing game.

LEVEL Intermediate—Advanced ☆ ★ ★

TIME Preparatory Disscussion: 20 minutes
Homework Assignment: N/A
Presentations: 3—5 minutes per student

PROCEDURE

— Intermediate Version —

01 In advance, the teacher writes down a short description of a country in preparation to tell the students. Be sure not to include the name of the country within since the students are to guess which country is being described to them.

02 Once the students have guessed successfully after listening to the description, tell the students that their homework assignment is to do the same. Each student is to pick a country (no more than two students should pick the same country) and write at least four sentences to describe it. They are to include location, customs, history, and a description of a scene in the country. Set the students up for success by handing out a model and then examining the sentence structure within. An intermediate example might read something like this:

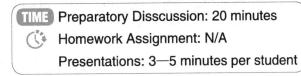

a. 我给大家介绍一个国家。

b. 这个国家在北半球，它的南面有蒙古、中国和一些别的国家，西面有
   不少欧洲国家。*(location)*

c. 这个国家的人们使用的文字很独特。*(language)*

d. 这个国家的人们有一个特别的习惯。冬天的时候，河边常常站着很多
   人，他们穿着游衣，准备跳进冰冷的河水中游泳。*(scene description)*

e. 这个国家历史上出现过不少世界著名的文学家和艺术家。*(history)*

f. 请你们猜一猜，这是哪个国家？

The students do not have to follow the model to a tee since the very
nature of the assignment requires writing existential sentences. However,
requiring them to describe a scene in the country will add variety to their
sentence structures.

—— Advanced Version ——

01

For advanced students, in addition to employing more complex sentence
structures, different subject matters can be chosen as well. For instance,
if your class readings cover travel spots in China, you might have the
students introduce a Chinese city. Just be sure that the students will be
familiar enough with the subject matter so that the "guessing" part of the
activity is feasible. Using a Chinese city as a subject, below is an example
of the advanced model.

a. 我给大家介绍一个中国的城市。

b. 这个城市位于中国的东北部，是黑龙江省的省会。*(location)*

c. 这个城市每到冬季就会举办冰雪节、冰灯博览会。*(custom)*

d. 这个城市最吸引人的是那里的异国情调。你们想象一下，城市里有很
   多欧式风格的建筑，街上铺着鹅卵石，霓虹灯下站着金发碧眼的美丽
   女郎，空中不时传来悠扬的歌声。*(scene description)*

e. 这个城市也被称为"东方莫斯科""东方小巴黎"。*(history)*

f. 你们能不能猜出这是哪个城市呢？

02 In addition, the assignment can be expanded to a full-length essay. Doing so provides an excellent opportunity to show real essays (pulled from the internet) written by Chinese students for similar assignments. Students are fascinated to see what their Chinese peers do in school. Moreover, progressing to the point where they can actually understand the writing of their Chinese peers is very encouraging indeed.

03 While correcting the students' homework, circle words that the class as a whole has not learned yet. When giving their presentations, students will write these words and their meanings on the board as they come to them—just as a teacher would do.

04 Once the papers have been handed back, give students time to digest them. Tell them that in the next class period they will present their essays—but with a key change. Clues are to be presented in the order of their difficulty with the most obvious clue stated last. This will prevent students from guessing right away once they hear where the country or city is located. The ultimate order, of course, will depend on what each student has written, but the location must be the last clue given.

Verbal Silliness

FOCUS Although serial verb constructions do not technically exist in English, students generally do not have too much trouble understanding this structure in Chinese. Since the consecutive verbs are simply following the natural order of events, the Chinese is intuitively easy to understand. In English, however, if a clause has two or more verbs, predication or a conjunction must be used. Learners of Chinese are often tempted to use 和 but that is pretty much the extent of their difficulty. The preliminary teaching part of the activity ensures students' grasp of serial verb structures; and the Chinese "Mad Libs" section, while not directly targeting serial verbs per se, helps students stem their predilection to overusing 和 to join clauses.

LEVEL Elementary ★ ☆ ☆

TIME Preliminary Teaching: 10—15 minutes
Mad Libs®: 20—25 minutes

PROCEDURE

—— Preliminary Teaching ——

01 Have students take a minute or two to write down as many Chinese verbs, along with their English definitions, that they can recall. Students can choose to use *pinyin* or characters.

02 Working in pairs, students exchange what each has written and discuss what each verb means.

03 Have each pair work together to make five sentences that contain a serial verb structure by using the verbs they have written down. Provide students with serial verb patterns and examples.

Pattern: Subject + Predicate 1 (+ Object 1) + Predicate 2 (+ Object 2)

Example: 我有一个问题问王老师。

04 Each pair is then asked to write on the board two sentences that they have made and present them to the whole class. Pairs can choose to present both sentences together or have each student present one sentence. After each sentence is presented, check for comprehension and highlight key features by asking questions.

—— Chinese "Mad Libs®" ——

Although grammar-based fill-in-the-blank games such as Mad Libs® are not particularly suitable for such a contextual language as Chinese, if kept very simple (and with some on-the-spot editing of the teacher when necessary), some memorable stories can be created.

01 The teacher writes up a simple story and deletes key words that can be substituted with words chosen by the students. For example:

a. 彼得很饿, 他去商店_____ (verb) 披萨。买了披萨以后, 他_____ (verb) 到家, 打开冰箱_____ (verb) 出一箱啤酒, 开始_____ (verb) 啤酒、_____ (verb) 披萨, 还一边_____ (verb) 电视。他_____ (verb) 了十二瓶啤酒、_____ (verb) 了六块披萨, _____ (verb) 了四个小时的电视。他吃了那么多东西, 很想睡觉。这时, 一个女的给他_____ (verb) 电话, 很生气地说: "你为什么跟玛丽一起_____ (verb) 啤酒、_____ (verb) 披萨、_____ (verb) 电视, _____ (verb) 得那么开心? " 彼得觉得很奇怪, 他一直一个人在家, 哪儿来的玛丽?

b. _____ (A male person) 很_____ (a feeling), 他去商店买_____ (noun)。买了_____ (noun) 以后, 他回到家, 在_____ (room) 里喝啤酒、看_____ (noun), 看了很久。他吃_____ (food) 吃得很多, 就_____ (a feeling) 了, 想睡觉。但是_____ (a female person) 给他打电话, 她很生气地说: "你为什么跟_____ (a person) 一起_____ (verb) 得那么开心? " _____ (The male person from first blank) 觉得很_____ (a feeling)。

02 Before class or while the students are busy taking a quiz or doing classwork, write the story on the board and cover it up with a screen or

97

some paper.

03 Ask the students for words that fit the parts of speech or categories that are missing. For example, "Give me a verb. Give me the name of a male person. Give me a noun...." Sometimes ask students for words as a group, and sometimes as individuals. Mix it up. If part of the board has room, write their chosen words there; otherwise just jot the words down on a piece of paper.

04 Uncover the story, and fill in the words. Read the story out loud together as a class. The story should sound ridiculous and hopefully provide memorable examples of various serial verb constructions.

38) Comma Pile-up

FOCUS While verbal stacking is particularly prevalent in Chinese, this linguistic phenomenon is not unique to the Chinese language and therefore feels rather familiar to Chinese language learners. There is, however, a serial or chain construction which is truly unique to Chinese: sentences with strings of clauses separated by commas. In contrast to Western languages, the 逗号 actively establishes the meaning of complex sentences. Accustomed to sentences having a clear subject and predicate with only non-essential clauses set aside by commas, Chinese language learners can get lost in seemingly never-ending Chinese sentences. This activity is designed to both introduce and practice Chinese sentence segmentation and the unique nature of Chinese complex sentences.

LEVEL Intermediate—Advanced ☆ ★ ★

TIME Preliminary Teaching: 15—20 minutes
In-Class Activity: 20—30 minutes

PROCEDURE

— Preliminary Teaching —

01 Explain to the students the structural difference between Chinese and English complex sentences. For instance, what is a well-written sentence in Chinese would be considered a run-on mess of a sentence in English. In Chinese, there exists distinct relationships between phrases within a complex sentence. While there is no need to get into the linguistic weeds, the following six "relationships" will be most helpful for students in improving both their reading and writing:

- 条件关系 (conditional relationship);

99

- 因果关系 (cause and effect relationship);

- 转折关系 (contrastive relationship);

- 选择关系 (preferential relationship);

- 递进关系 (progressive relationship);

- 总结关系 (summary relationship)

02 Once you have introduced the Chinese comma and its uses, be sure to ask the students, "What does this comma express?" while going over class readings. At this point, a topical essay assignment would be appropriate. The students will be delighted to find that their compositions now have a much more authentic Chinese flavor.

── In-Class Activity ──

01 The teacher thinks of topics which can be elaborated upon and puts them on cards. A good mix of serious and frivolous topics works well.

02 Divide the class into teams of three to five students. Have each team pick a topic card. Each team's task is to expound on the subject by writing six complex sentences using the "relationships" gone over previously. Their sentences must flow from one to the other in a somewhat logical, albeit possibly forced, fashion. For example, for the topic 幽默, students might come up with something like the following:

- 幽默，是一个很复杂的现象，也是一个很神秘的东西。

- 同样的笑话，有些人觉得有趣，而有些人则觉得乏味，甚至感受到冒犯。

- 每个人的价值观和生活经历以及宗教信仰不相同，所以每个人的反应也不一样。

- 怪不得当喜剧演员看观众的时候，会发现总有一些冷淡的面孔。

- 只要有半数观众笑了，喜剧演员就十分满足。

- 总的来说，虽然研究人员还不太了解幽默这个现象，但可以肯定的是，大多数人都喜欢哈哈大笑。

Obviously, by the intermediate and advanced stages there is a great disparity in ability among the students. Keep that in mind when forming groups. Try to ensure that each student, no matter how weak, contributes a sentence—or at least part of a sentence.

03 When the teams are finished, they are to write their "six-sentence exposition" on the board. As each team reads theirs, highlight the good points and ask for suggestions on how to make some sentences even better. The teams vote on which team did the best job.

Bǎ Basics

FOCUS A good argument can be made to cover bǎ, such an important feature of Chinese, early in the students' studies. Too often learners of Chinese find themselves after years of studying unable to ask someone to move or place an object somewhere else—which is a quite common request in daily life. Students need a lot of spaced repetition of the bǎ structure to become comfortable with its use so the longer they are at it, the better. Below are ideas on how to methodically introduce students to the bǎ structure early on. In addition, a spirited game of "Who Killed Mr. So-and-So?" in which bǎ is used, but not explicitly emphasized, adds some good variety to classic exercises and order-and-response drills. The game also has them practice the " 在⋯⋯ (处所) 里 / 外 / 上 / 下 " structure, which is another troublesome spot and that often coincides with bǎ— and thus tackles two difficulties in one.

LEVEL Elementary—Intermediate ★ ★ ☆   **TIME** 15—20 minutes

PROCEDURE

—— Preliminary Practice ——

01 An efficient way to introduce the bǎ structure is to start off with a command. For instance, 请把娃娃放在桌子上. Make the object a memorable one. 娃娃 works well because to foreign ears it sounds somewhat silly, and therefore more likely to stick in the students' brains.

02 Write the sentence on the board in *pinyin*, characters, and Chinglish (please "take" doll put at table on). Randomly hand the doll to individual students and ask them to put it on the table. Once the students have caught on, mix it up by asking them to put the doll on the floor, put the doll under the table, put the doll in the bag, etc. Then have them throw the doll around and order their fellow students around.

03 Afterwards, have a more formal lesson on the bǎ structure. It is better to keep these lessons brief, but have them more often. For instance, in one lesson you might simply have the students convert straight SVO sentences into bǎ sentences. In another lesson, you might go over the rules governing the use of bǎ. And then later on have students find the errors in "sick" bǎ sentences with grammatical errors.

04 While covering other material during your lessons if you notice a student doing something that could be described with bǎ, interrupt the class and ask everyone what that person just did. Spaced repetition is effective so don't hesitate to take advantage of an opportunity to ask a student to 请把门打开, etc.

—— Further Reinforcement ——

01 Take pictures that show a series of actions performed by someone. For instance, a man in different stages of setting a table, or a person decorating their apartment.

02 Prepare a handout and have students work in pairs to describe the pictures. *(See Sample.)*

03 A lively alternative is for the students to take a series of pictures and have their classmates describe the actions shown within.

Sample

张三刚搬进一间公寓，他想装饰一下客厅，所以买了一些家具和装饰品回来。以下图片记录了他所做的一些事情。用"把"字句，即"S + 把 + N + V + 在 + Place + 里 / 外 / 上 / 下"和"放、挂、摆"等动词，跟你的同伴讨论并回答以下两个问题：

1. 张三做了什么事情？

2. 张三的行为产生了什么结果或影响？

问题：张三把中国画怎么了？现在中国画在哪里？

答案：_____

问题：张三把地毯怎么了？现在地毯在哪里？

答案：_____

问题：张三把茶几怎么了？现在茶几在哪里？

答案：_____

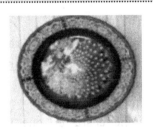 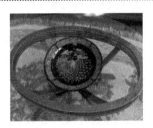

问题：张三把花盆怎么了？现在花盆在哪里？

答案：_____

问题：张三把花怎么了？现在花在哪里？

答案：_____

——Who Killed Mr. So-and-So? ——

This activity is based on the board game Clue® in which players try to deduce who murdered the victim, the location of the crime, and the weapon used. Most Western students are very familiar with the game. While considerable set-up preparation is required, once the materials are created, they can be reused over and over again.

SET-UP

01 First, prepare a worksheet which lists six suspects, six rooms, and six weapons. *(See Sample A.)*

02 Then for each group of students prepare a set of cards with one card for each suspect, room, and weapon. There should be a total of 18 cards for each group. *(See Sample B.)*

03 To save class time, the teacher may remove one "character," one "room," and one "weapon" card from each set of cards and place them in their own envelope before class. These cards are the solution to the murder mystery. Shuffle the remaining 15 cards in the set, clip them together, and then put them in the same envelope. This is just to ensure that each separate set stays together until you distribute the packets in class.

PROCEDURE

01 Hand out a copy of the worksheet to each student. Divide the class into groups with the maximum being five in each one.

02 Each group receives one envelope. They are not to look inside. The teacher removes the clipped cards from the envelope and distributes these remaining cards to that particular group face-down.

03 One student starts by attempting to guess "Who did it?," "In what room?," and "With what weapon?" For instance, after looking at his cards, the first student makes an educated guess and perhaps says: "王医生在书房里用刀把他杀死了。" If the student to his left has any one of those cards, he must secretly show the guesser one—and only one—of those cards. Once one student has shown the guesser one card, the guesser's turn ends. Now it is the next student's turn to make a guess, and so forth.

04 For each group, the winner is the student who, after making a guess, no one is able to show a card. Check the envelope for confirmation.

Sample A

人物 rénwù (character)

白太太 Bái tàitai (Mrs. Bai)	
刘先生 Liú xiānsheng (Mr. Liu)	
黄律师 Huáng lùshī (Lawyer Huang)	
王医生 Wáng yīshēng (Dr. Wang)	
李教授 Lǐ jiàoshòu (Professor Li)	
林经理 Lín jīnglǐ (Manager Lin)	

地点 dìdiǎn (place)

书房 shūfáng (study)	
厨房 chúfáng (kitchen)	
卧室 wòshì (bedroom)	
客厅 kètīng (living room)	
院子 yuànzi (garden)	
浴室 yùshì (bathroom)	

武器 wǔqì (weapon)	
杯子 bēizi (glass)	
花瓶 huāpíng (vase)	
毒药 dúyào (poison)	
绳子 shéngzi (rope)	
石头 shítou (rock)	
烛台 zhútái (candlestick)	

Sample B

Suspects

Bái tàitai
白太太

Liú xiānsheng
刘先生

Huáng lùshī
黄律师

Wáng yīshēng
王医生

Lǐ jiàoshòu
李教授

Lín jīnglǐ
林经理

Rooms

shūfáng

书房

chúfáng

厨房

wòshì

卧室

kètīng

客厅

yuànzi

院子

yùshì

浴室

Weapons

bēizi
杯子

huāpíng
花瓶

dúyào
毒药

shéngzi
绳子

shítou
石头

zhútái
烛台

谁在<u>哪个房间</u>里用<u>什么武器</u>把他杀死了?

<u>a person</u> zài <u>a room</u> lǐ yòng <u>a weapon</u> bǎ tā shā sǐ le?

ACTIVITY 40

Verbal Lego

FOCUS This activity is for students who are just shy of becoming fully comfortable with the bǎ structure. A good idea is to preface this activity with a brief review of why some sentences using bǎ are simply just emphasizing the impact of the verbal action on the object, while other sentences, which contain action verbs and 到 or 在, must use bǎ. And since repetition is the key of all learning, "Verbal Lego" certainly has enough of that.

LEVEL Intermediate—Advanced ☆ ★ ★

TIME Preparation: 15—20 minutes
Lego Project Building: 20 minutes for each side in a pair

PROCEDURE

— Preparation —

01 To prepare, the teacher must have a box of Legos. A medium box of Classic Legos works well. In the instruction booklet, look at the objects that can be made with the set. Keeping in mind how you will be dividing the class into groups of no more than three students, select constructions that would be appropriate. For instance, weaker students should be given easier objects, and stronger students given more complex objects.

02 From the internet, download the illustrated instructions for each chosen object. Since you will be color copying, you will want to keep the handouts to a minimum to keep down costs. "Screen shot" the instructions and reduce them to fit comfortably on letter-sized paper. By doing so, even the most complex objects will require only two pages.

03 Build the objects yourself. After you are done, break them apart and put the necessary Lego pieces for each object in its own separate plastic bag.

04 Make a handout which contains the key vocabulary that the students will need when making their objects. *(See Sample.)*

—— In-Class Building ——

01 Write 把 on the board and then pass out the handout. Explain to the students that they will be divided into groups and must verbally explain to others how to make a Lego object—using Chinese.

02 Very briefly go over the handout, and then ask the students how they would say the following in Chinese:

- Grab a blue cube. (拿一块蓝色的正方体。)

- Put it on the top. (把它放在上面。)

- Shift it to the left a bit. (把它往左边挪一点儿)。

03 Divide the students into their groups and hand out the appropriate instructions to each group. Give the students 15 minutes or so to figure out (and write down) how they are going to verbally give the instructions.

04 Then pass out the appropriate Lego bags to each group, and announce the groups that are paired up with each other. So in each pair, one group gives the instructions first, and the other group builds. Then they switch roles.

NOTE

Use your own judgment regarding time. What works well is to give them preparation time and then leave enough time in the same class to have one group in each pair be able to finish making their object or come close to doing so. At the end of class, collect the Lego bags, including those which are unfinished. The students can finish up during the next class.

Sample

Vocabulary List A: Verbs

放	fàng	put
挪	núo	shift
拿	ná	grab, take
递	dì	pass

Vocabulary List B: Location

上面	shàngmian	top
下面	xiàmian	below
左边	zuǒbian	left
右边	yòubian	right
中间	zhōngjiān	middle

Vocabulary List C: Shapes

正方形	zhèngfāngxíng	square
正方体	zhèngfāngtǐ	cube
长方形	chángfāngxíng	rectangle
长方体	chángfāngtǐ	cuboid
圆形	yuánxíng	circle
圆柱体	yuánzhùtǐ	cylinder
十字形	shízìxíng	cross

Vocabulary List D: Colors

绿色	lǜsè	green
蓝色	lánsè	blue
红色	hóngsè	red
黄色	huángsè	yellow
橙色	chéngsè	orange
粉色	fěnsè	pink
紫色	zǐsè	purple
棕色	zōngsè	brown
浅	qiǎn	light
深	shēn	dark

ACTIVITY 41

Bad Acts

FOCUS It comes as no surprise to Chinese language teachers that both bǎ and bèi are tricky points for Chinese language learners. Yet, the grammatical relationship between bǎ and bèi fortunately gives teachers further opportunity to deepen students' understanding of these two voice markers—and new ways to practice them. This activity does just that by having students manipulate sentences into both active and passive voice, thereby helping students further increase their facility with these unique prepositions.

LEVEL Intermediate—Advanced ☆ ★ ★   **TIME** 20—30 minutes

PROCEDURE

01 Conduct a quick review of bǎ and bèi with fill-in-the-blank warm-up exercises. For example:

- 他被对手打倒了。(Bèi could be replaced with bǎ, but the meaning would be dramatically altered.)

- 我把礼物给刘老师了。(Bǎ cannot be replaced with bèi.)

- 飞机票被我弄丢了。(Bèi cannot be replaced with bǎ, but the sentence could be restructured into a bǎ sentence.)

This is a great opportunity to include everyday practical verbs (such as 搞, 弄, 挪 etc.) that often get short shrift in standard textbooks.

02 Divide the class into three teams. Each team is to think of three actions, which they will later act out, that can be described with both bǎ and bèi. For instance: a student hits the other; two students steal something of another; students perform a benign yet odd act such as putting the teacher's chair on a desk, etc. Have the students write their sentences down in both bǎ and bèi forms so that the teacher can check on each team's progress.

03 For the first round, select which team will be the acting team, the bǎ team, and the bèi team. The bǎ and bèi teams will stand near the board. After the acting team performs their action, the bǎ and bèi teams each will write down a sentence that describes the action using the "voice marker" of their respective team. A point is awarded for each correct sentence.

04 After the acting team has performed their three actions, the teams rotate. That is, the "bǎ team" becomes the new "acting team"; the "bèi team" becomes the "bǎ team"; and the previous "acting team" is now the "bèi team." Keep going until all teams have rotated through all three roles.

Our Worst Day Ever

FOCUS "Practice makes perfect," so the saying goes. However, practicing the bèi construction can often lead to its overuse by students who accustomed to the frequency of the passive voice in their native tongue often desire in error to make Chinese sentences into passive ones. For example: While "Credit cards are accepted by the bank" is right on the money in English, Chinese prefers 银行接受了我的信用卡 over its passive counterpart 我的信用卡被银行接受了. This activity is aimed at practicing bèi, but at the same time driving the point home that the passive voice in Chinese is often, albeit not always, associated with negative events.

LEVEL Intermediate—Advanced ☆ ★ ★   **TIME** 20—30 minutes ⏱

PROCEDURE

01 The teacher first divides the students into pairs, or teams of three, and then tells the students that they are in a competition to write down the worst possible day that they could have.

02 Working as a team, they are to write a short story describing their fictional "Worst Day Ever." The challenge is that their story must have at least ten bèi sentences.

03 At this point, a quick review of the bèi sentence structure using examples would be helpful. Be sure to include sentences with the "doer" of the verb's action known and unknown. For example, 电脑被弟弟弄坏了 and 电脑被（人）弄坏了.

04 When the students are finished, the teams read their stories out loud to each other. The class then votes to determine which team had the "Worst Day Ever."

NOTE

Depending on class size and students' interest level, this activity can be spread over two class periods: one for writing; and the other for judging.

ACTIVITY 43) Rap Chatter

FOCUS This activity serves as students' first introduction to the Topic-Comment structure of Chinese. Try to keep it light, interesting—and brief.

LEVEL Elementary ★ ☆ ☆

TIME Preliminary Teaching: 15 minutes
Rap Chatter: 15—20 minutes

PROCEDURE

—— Preliminary Teaching ——

01 The teacher writes questions, which are in "topic-comment" format, on the board. For example:

> 你，怎么样?
> 你妹妹，怎么样?
> 我明天请你吃饭，怎么样?

02 Pose the questions to individual students and, if necessary, guide them to a correct answer. Then write their answers on the board. For example:

Topic-Comment Questions	Guided Students' Answers
你，怎么样?	我，很好。/ 我，累死了。/ 我，马马虎虎。
你妹妹，怎么样?	我妹妹，她很忙。/ 我妹妹，她很好。
我明天请你吃饭，怎么样?	你明天请我吃饭，太好了！/ 你明天请我吃饭，对不起，我没有时间！

03 Ask the students to identify the subjects and main verbs in the answers. Once they have expressed confusion, briefly explain that Chinese is a "topic-comment" language whereas English is a language in which every sentence must have both a clear subject and a clear verb.

04 Now ask the students to translate the following sentence into English.

鸡，吃了。

Explain that context determines whether the sentence means "The chicken ate" or "The chicken was eaten."

05 There is no need to get into the linguistic weeds here. Point out that the topic-comment structure makes speaking Chinese easier. One must simply state what one wants to talk about and then add a comment.

NOTE

By the way, English does something similar when introductory umbrella clauses are used. For example:

As for economics (topic), John (subject) prefers (verb) Milton Friedman's ideas.

—— Rap Chatter ——

01 Working in pairs, have the students write a six-line rap using the "topic-comment" structure. To give students some ideas, provide them with an example:

Student A: 看电影，怎么样?

Student B: 看电影，很不好!

Student A: 很不好? 为什么?

Student B: 看电影，太麻烦!

Student A: 太麻烦？为什么？

Student B: 为什么？没时间！

 When the students are ready (or time is up), have each pair perform in front of the class.

This, I Don't Agree!

FOCUS In a classroom setting, students have little difficulty in understanding the topic-comment structure of Chinese, but what they may not realize (especially if they are in a non-immersion environment) is how this peculiarity of Chinese facilitates speaking. There is no need for them to organize an entire sentence in their brains beforehand. Just state the topic (give your brain a break), and then comment on it. Since a debate lends itself to using this structure even in their mother tongue, it is just the thing needed for students to realize that they can, indeed, use Chinese to speak about sophisticated topics.

LEVEL Intermediate—Advanced ☆ ★ ★

TIME Preparation & Homework: N/A
Debate: 30—40 minutes

PROCEDURE

— Preparation & Homework —

01 First, think of appropriate debate topics. It is best to have a series of debates spread throughout the course. Ideally debate topics should be related to course material, if not directly then tangentially, by covering vocabulary that would be useful while debating that particular issue. If nothing from your current course materials will work, then supplement it with a modified newspaper article, etc.

02 Once the topic is decided, explain to the students that they will be having a debate on that topic. Their homework is to prepare a sheet listing the pros and cons of the argument. Since you want them to spend the bulk of their time framing their Chinese arguments, rather than on thinking or researching in their native tongue, give them guidance by breaking down the issue further. For instance, let's say the debate is "汉字简化：利大于弊还是弊大于利？" Ask them to divide their pro and con arguments into sections. In this example, you could ask them to make pro and con arguments that would cover the cultural, aesthetic, practical, and political dimensions of the issue.

03 While correcting their homework, jot down the particular good points that each student made. After you hand back their work, discuss it fully to help them prepare for the upcoming debate. Let's say someone made an argument in favor of the higher aesthetic quality of traditional characters by mentioning that luxury brands often use traditional characters to sell their products. Ask the other students how they would counter that. If you know someone made the argument that calligraphy scripts are in essence traditional characters, call on that student.

04 When covering all the arguments and counter-arguments, highlight how they can break down what they want to say into simple topic-comment statements.

05 In preparation for the debate, also hand out a previously prepared list of handy sayings used in debates. *(See Sample.)* Tell the students that each person must use at least two of these phrases during the course of the debate.

—— The Big Debate ——

01 Ask one team which side they want to debate. Let's say they say "正方." If you flip a coin and it lands on "heads," then they can indeed argue the Pro position. If the coin lands on "tails," then the other team gets to choose to be either "反方" or "正方."

02 Start the debate with a hammed-up formal introduction along the lines of "各位嘉宾，欢迎大家参加今天的辩论会……" And begin the actual debate by posing a specific question to the pro team. From then on, act as a moderator to ensure a good give and take, and participation of all students. When the students are stumbling, help them out by providing a handy "topic" to begin their statement. When all the various arguments have been made, close the debate.

Sample

- **陈述观点　Stating an Opinion**

  我的意见是……　In my opinion, ...

  我个人认为……　Personally I think...

  就我而言，……　As far as I'm concerned, ...

- **质疑观点　Challenging an Opinion**

  那不可能是真的。　That can't be true.

  但关于……方面呢？　But what about...?

- **重申观点　Clarifying a Point**

  我刚才说的是……　What I said was...

  我的意思是说……　What I meant to say was...

  让我重申刚才所说的。　Let me rephrase what I said.

- 同意观点　**Agreeing with an Opinion**

  我也这样认为。　I think so too.

  我完全赞同。　I agree completely.

  我完全同意你所说的。　I agree with you entirely.

- 反对意见　**Disagreeing with an Opinion**

  我不那样认为。　I don't think so.

  我无法同意你的观点。　I can't possibly agree with your opinion.

  我不想反对你，但……　I hate to disagree with you, but...

Voidable Subjects

ACTIVITY 45

FOCUS Beginning Chinese language learners are often overwhelmed with *pinyin*, characters, and tones. All is so new. Therefore, it is best not to burden them with too much extraneous information. Linguistic finer points can wait—perhaps, indefinitely. Yet, every now and then when there is concern that comprehension is lagging behind, highlighting the differences between Chinese and English may be helpful. This activity brings to the fore Chinese's contextual versus English's grammatical nature.

 **LEVEL** Elementary ★ ☆ ☆

 **TIME** 15 minutes

PROCEDURE

01 The students are divided into groups of varying abilities. Have them read a passage that they are learning or have learned. For example:

> 小李是大学三年级的学生，她天天都很忙，每天除了要上四节课以外，还得在图书馆工作三个小时，有时中午没有时间吃饭就去上课了，下课以后常常要跟同学一起讨论功课、做作业。这个学期她一共有六门课，电脑和中文课作业很多，也很不容易，她每天都要忙到半夜一点才睡觉。

02 Have students work together to look for the subject of each sentence in the passage. If a subject cannot be found where one would be expected, they are to put a zero pronoun there, i.e., Ø.

03 Then have them go through the passage again and determine who or what each zero pronoun is referring to.

04 As a class, go over the passage and make note of the differences between Chinese and English.

When You Assume...

FOCUS Context is essential in the Chinese language. As such, making inferences from context is something that Chinese language learners must become accustomed to doing. This often poses a challenge, however, for native speakers of highly grammatical languages such as English, in which making assumptions, while not strictly verboten, is frowned upon. This activity is aimed at building awareness of the contextual nature of Chinese. After such awareness is built, classroom comprehension checks on readings which contain zero pronouns and topic chains become all the more meaningful to the students.

LEVEL Intermediate—Advanced ☆ ★ ★   **TIME** 20—30 minutes ⏱

PROCEDURE

01 The teacher prepares an appropriately-sized dialogue that will fit on the board and is tailored to the students' current level. The text should be cluttered with "overt" pronouns and "repeated" topics which in Chinese are not necessary for, and if anything hinder, comprehension. It should sound awkward. In the example below, the "overt" pronouns and "repeated" topics are in bold.

A: 老板看见记者了吗?

B: **他**看见**他**了。

A: **他的**情绪怎么样?

B: **他**愤怒得说不出话来。

A: **我**不能怪他, 今天早上**我**在报纸上看到一篇文章, **文章**说我们公司面临不少困难, **我们**不能偿还贷款, **公司**快倒闭了。

B: 我真讨厌记者们。

A: 你说得对，我也不喜欢他们。

02 First, you will want to briefly explain why Chinese language learners often overuse pronouns. An efficient way to do so is by using the following example.*

我们在中国学习的时候，一点儿玩的时间都没有，每天除了学习就是学习，有时候连睡觉的时间都没有。

While we were studying in China, (we) did not have any time for playing. Every day, (we) studied, and then studied some more. Sometimes (we) didn't even have enough time to sleep.

First read the Chinese. But before doing so, ask the students to count how many times you say 我们. Then before reading the English version, ask the students to note how many times you say "we." The point that Chinese is a context-based as opposed to a grammar-based language has been clearly made.

03 Now divide the class into two teams. Alternating sides, a representative from each team is to erase an "overt" pronoun or "repeated" topic from the dialogue you have previously written on the board. Only those pronouns and topics which can be erased without disintegrating the meaning of the text are permissible. If a team erases a particular pronoun or topic that is vital for continuity, they lose a point.

04 Throughout the activity, be sure that students understand why a particular "overt" pronoun or "repeated" topic can or cannot be deleted. Ask questions such as, "What is X referring back to?" Read the text again as a class and clarify any trouble spots for the students.

---

* Example from Xing, J. Z. *Teaching and Learning Chinese as a Foreign Language: A Pedagogical Grammar*. Hong Kong: Hong Kong University Press, 2006.

NOTE

Another option is to select a chapter or so of a popular Western children's book which has been translated into Chinese. Modify a small portion of it by adding the unstated pronouns and topics. Write that particular portion on the board and run through the activity. Once the activity is done, hand out the chapter in both Chinese and English. Odds are the students will be raring to read it.

Chapter 6
Putting It All Together

In this chapter, we aim to raise students' linguistic and cultural competence by having them use the language in the real world. In particular, students are encouraged to access technology to either review, or to enhance oral and written proficiency at the discourse level. Four activities are presented here:

Review Games

FOCUS While Confucius most definitely didn't have Jeopardy® or Bingo in mind when he asked 学而时习之，不亦说乎？, these two review games have been popular among American students and teachers alike for decades for that very reason. They are wonderful additions at the conclusion of a course or after significant material has been covered that warrants review. Prizes for the winners are a nice touch, however, the real prize truly is the sense of accomplishment that comes from the clear illustration of the long-term progress that the students have made.

LEVEL Elementary—Advanced ★ ★ ★

TIME 30 minutes per activity

PROCEDURE

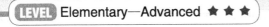

— Jeopardy® (Elementary, PowerPoint Version) —

This version differs from the popular American television quiz show in both rules and format. Unlike the latter, which requires the individual contestents to give the answer in the form of a question, this version requires a team to translate an English sentence into Chinese.

01 The teacher prepares appropriate materials for review: vocabulary, grammar, and texts.

02 To develop your own version of Jeopardy®, scan the QR code to download a PowerPoint template and follow the steps below:

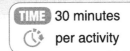

a. Pull up the downloadable Jeopardy® PPT template provided by the authors. On Slide 3, modify the categories on top in accordance with your curriculum. The material underneath is arranged in order from easiest to hardest. The greater the difficulty, the more points awarded.

b. Right-mouse click 100 or 200, and then select "Edit Hyperlink" to understand the relationship between each slide.

c. Starting on Slide 4, replace the English sentences with ones appropriate for your course of study. Appropriate graphics can be integrated as well.

d. When all is set, save the file as a PowerPoint presentation. It is now ready to use.

03   Divide the class into three or four teams with three students in each.

04   Explain the four rules of the game:

a. The task is to orally translate the English sentences presented into Chinese.

b. When the team is ready with their translation, one student gives the answer on behalf of the team. Team members should take turns being the representative.

c. If the team fails to answer before the music is over, the first person on any of the opposing teams to raise his or her hand can answer.

d. The team with the most amount of money wins.

05   During the game, the teacher records the score, points out crucial errors, and, if necessary, leads the class to repeat the Chinese sentences correctly.

06   Award each student a prize with the winning ones receiving different items for special encouragement.

—— Jeopardy® (Intermediate-Advanced, Non-Electronic Version) ——

At this stage, break away from formal language learning, and run it as a classic knowledge game. Using Chinese to play a game testing students' basic knowledge is the ultimate test of their Chinese ability! The students will be delighted when they actually pull it off.

01 In advance, the teacher thinks of several categories and then prepares six answers and their respective clues which will elicit those answers. For each category arrange the answer and clue combinations according to their level of difficulty. Assign points to be awarded to each. Write these down on a reference sheet to be used during the game.

02 Below is a sample of two categories with their respective answers which was appropriate for an intermediate class who had also been lightly introduced to Chinese history and thought.

动物

分值	提示	答案
100 分	人类最好的朋友	狗
200 分	会抓老鼠	猫
300 分	生活在水里；会游泳	鱼
400 分	在公园里能听到它们的叫声；会飞	鸟
500 分	很聪明；喜欢吃香蕉	猴子
600 分	代表中国的动物	熊猫

名人

分值	提示	答案
100 分	中国男演员，武打明星，出演过《尖峰时刻》等电影。	成龙
200 分	中国篮球运动员，曾经为休斯敦火箭队打球。	姚明
300 分	中国女演员，出演过《卧虎藏龙》等电影。	章子怡
400 分	中国著名的思想家，名言：知之为知之，不知为不知，是知也。	孔子
500 分	中国历史上第一位使用"皇帝"称号的君主。	秦始皇
600 分	中国著名的思想家，名言：道可道，非常道。	老子

Be sure that the clues largely contain vocabulary which the students have learned. When using new vocabulary is unavoidable, make sure the clue is obvious enough that even without knowing a particular word or two, the clue is still decipherable. As for the answers, this is a great time to include previously covered material. The value of which was also discussed in the activity "Query Challenges".

03 On the day of the class, write the names of the categories on individual sheets of colored paper held horizontally. Tape them across on the board. Underneath each one, write down the amount of points allotted. For example:

动物	名人
100 分	100 分
200 分	200 分
300 分	300 分
400 分	400 分
500 分	500 分
600 分	600 分

04 Select a student to go first. They are to choose a category and then an amount. Erase the appropriate amount and then read the clue. Give the student a reasonable amount of time to come up with the answer. There is no need for students to state the answer in the form of a question as is done in the Jeopardy television show. For more advanced students, doing so might be appropriate if the knowledge game is on the easy side.

05 If the student answers correctly, they are to add the points to their personal tally. If the student cannot answer or answers incorrectly, the first student to raise their hand can "steal" it and try to answer. The first student to get it right can add the points to their *own* tally.

06 The turn to select a category and amount goes to the next student, and so forth. The student with the most amount of points wins. Award prizes for the top three highest totals.

—— Bingo (Intermediate-Advanced) ——

Translating sentences from one's mother tongue into the foreign language being studied—not the other way around—is a remarkably effective exercise. No wonder it is the common tried and true learning tool of successful language learners. See to it that your students make this sort of practice an integral part of their studying.

01 Think of several grammar or other key points appropriate for review. For example: Action Verbs; Adjectives; Noun Phrases; Comparisons; Questions; When...; Before...; After...; Bǎ; etc. To lighten it up, throw in some more generic ones such as Handy Sayings or Fancy Sentence Structures as general hodepodge categories. Five to nine categories work well. Then for each category prepare eight or more sentences/phrases for each section. Create a handout for your use during the game and then for later distribution.

02 Using a letter-sized sheet of paper, prepare a bingo sheet with 8 squares across and 8 squares down. In each square, type in one review category. Be sure that each line formed, whether it be down, across or diagonal has at least five different categories within. *(See Sample.)*

03 Select a student to pick the first category. Using your handout, read one of the sentences/phrases from the appropriate category. The student then must translate what you have just said. For longer or more difficult sentences/phrases, write down the student's response on the board.

04 If the student is correct, they can put an "✕" in the corresponding square of their choosing. For example, if the student chose "Comparisons," they could mark any one square with "Comparisons" written within. If the student is wrong, the first student with the correct answer to raise their hand gets to mark off the corresponding square on their sheet.

The next student selects, and so forth. The first student to "×" off eight squares in a row wins.

Afterwards, pass out copies of your handout. A good idea is to conduct timed translation quizzes over the course of several class periods. Covering two categories per quiz, give the students five minutes to translate as many as they can of the 16 sentences.

Sample

Action Verbs	Adjectives	Handy Sayings	Questions	把	Adjectives	Noun Phrases	COM-PARISONS
Adjectives	把	COM-PARISONS	Action Verbs	Before...	Noun Phrases	When...	Adjectives
Noun Phrases	COM-PARISONS	Handy Sayings	Adjectives	把	COM-PARISONS	Action Verbs	Noun Phrases
COM-PARISONS	After...	把	Noun Phrases	COM-PARISONS	Questions	Adjectives	Handy Sayings
Questions	Action Verbs	After...	把	COM-PARISONS	Handy Sayings	Noun Phrases	Noun Phrases
把	Noun Phrases	Action Verbs	When...	Action Verbs	Handy Sayings	COM-PARISONS	Action Verbs
Adjectives	Action Verbs	Action Verbs	Handy Sayings	Adjectives	Noun Phrases	COM-PARISONS	把
When···	COM-PARISONS	Noun Phrases	Action Verbs	Adjectives	Questions	把	COM-PARISONS

Dear Diary...

FOCUS Compositional writing practice in foreign language classrooms is often frustrating for students and teachers alike. Students' papers are riddled with too many errors (which might well lead to fossilization of said errors) and too much of the students' time is spent on silent brainstorming in their mother tongue, even before pen is put to paper.

These pitfalls can be mostly avoided in two ways: (1) Create writing assignments that students can accomplish with what they know now. Aim high for reading assignments (input) and aim lower for writing assignments (output). Naturally, students' output will always be lagging behind their input. (2) Give the students samples from which to model their own writing. Don't worry, they won't blindly copy and simply substitute key words. In fact, by giving them some structure and highlighting sentence patterns, you free them up to express themselves more or less correctly and confidently.

While keeping a journal is particularly effective in foreign language learning, we need to be aware that not all personalities take to it. The key here is to provide enough structure and some creative variations which will make writing journal entries more palatable for those who are resistent.

LEVEL Elementary—Advanced ★ ★ ★

TIME In-Class Practice/Discussion: 15 minutes
Homework: N/A

PROCEDURE

— Structured Basic Version —

01 Ask the students to write five sentences to describe a particular day of theirs in *pinyin* or characters. Be sure to provide them with some patterns and examples as shown below:

Pattern 1: Time (+ 是) + Time

Example 1: 今天是星期一。

Pattern 2: S + Adj

Example 2: 我很忙。

Pattern 3: S + V (+ O)

Example 3: 我有五节课。

Pattern 4: 因为 S + V (+ O), 所以 (S) + V (+ O)

Example 4: 因为我有五节课，所以没吃饭。

Pattern 5: Time + S + 才 + V (+ O)

Example 5: 四点半下课以后我才吃了一个汉堡。

02 Then have students download diary apps to their smart phones or iPads.

03 Guide students with entering in what they just wrote. Provide special help to those who are having difficulty with character entry. For some, handwriting may be more helpful. Depending on the application, this is a good opportunity to go over how to enter Chinese using *pinyin*, as well as how to use a stylus or mouse to write Chinese.

04 Encourage students, through bonus points, to jot down a few lines daily about any thoughts, or ideas they may have, or an interesting person they have encountered, etc.

05 As this is a personal assignment, allow flexibility for different abilities and personalities. In addition, suggest daily topics to help the more hesitant students to write a sentence or two. For instance, "What is your worst class and why?" "What would sports star × × do today?" and so forth.

─── Intermediate & Advanced Version ───

Diaries or journals are not just for teenage girls; key historical figures have written down their thoughts on a more or less daily basis. A fun way to break the barrier is to have the students model their journals or autobiographies on those of famous figures. A great choice is Benjamin Franklin's, which is one of the most charming autobiographies ever written.

01 Go over a level-appropriate modified Chinese translation of Benjamin Franklin's *Autobiography* that covers his attempt at moral perfection at the age of 20. *(See Sample*.)*

02 Starting with the first virtue "temperance," have the students spend the week writing their daily success or failure with this virtue. The next week, select another virtue, and so forth. Obviously, the twelfth virtue "chastity" should be excluded from the assignment. To guarantee good-humor and class camaraderie, the teacher should participate too. Once a week, have the class share their experiences.

03 End the three-month project by reading Franklin's own reflections at the age of 79 on his quest for moral perfection:

> 虽然我从来没有达到我原先雄心勃勃地想要达到的完善境界，而且还差得很远，但是我却凭借努力使我比不做这些尝试要好得多快乐得多。

Tho' I never arrived at the perfection I had been so ambitious of obtaining, but fell far short of it, yet I was, by the endeavour, a better and a happier man than I otherwise should have been if I had not attempted it.

---

* The sample is selected from *The Autobiography of Benjamin Franklin* and translated by the author with deletion and revision.

……我提出了十三种德行，这些是我当时认为有必要而且是适宜的全部德行，在每一项下面我加了一些简单的说明，进一步说明了我对这一德行的理解。

一、节制。吃饭不要过饱，饮酒不要过量。

二、谨言。不说于人于己都不利的话，避免闲言碎语。

三、秩序。把每一件物品都放在应该放的地方，做事井然有序。

四、决心。该做的事一定要做，要做的事必须做好。

五、节俭。所有花费必须利己或利人，不能浪费。

六、勤勉。珍惜时间，做有益的事，不做无益的事。

七、真诚。不要欺骗别人，思考问题要公正合理，发表看法要依据事实。

八、公平。不损人利己，要履行应尽的义务。

九、中庸。避免极端，学会容忍。

十、清洁。保持身体、衣着和住所的清洁卫生。

十一、宁静。不为琐事或不可避免的事而烦躁不安。

十二、略。

十三、谦虚。效仿耶稣和苏格拉底。

...and I included under thirteen names of virtues all that at that time occurred to me as necessary or desirable, and annexed to each a short precept, which fully expressed the extent I gave to its meaning.

These names of virtues, with their precepts were:

1. TEMPERANCE. Eat not to dullness; drink not to elevation.

2. SILENCE. Speak not but what may benefit others or yourself; avoid trifling conversation.

3. ORDER. Let all your things have their places; let each part of your business have its time.

4. RESOLUTION. Resolve to perform what you ought; perform without fail what you resolve.

5. FRUGALITY. Make no expense but to do good to others or yourself, i.e., waste nothing.

6. INDUSTRY. Lose no time; be always employed in something useful; cut off all unnecessary actions.

7. SINCERITY. Use no hurtful deceit; think innocently and justly, and, if you speak, speak accordingly.

8. JUSTICE. Wrong none by doing injuries or omitting the benefits that are your duty.

9. MODERATION. Avoid extremes; forbear resenting injuries so much as you think they deserve.

10. CLEANLINESS. Tolerate no uncleanliness in body, clothes, or habitation.

11. TRANQUILLITY. Be not disturbed at trifles, or at accidents common or unavoidable.

12. Omitted.

13. HUMILITY. Imitate Jesus and Socrates.

Open Notebook

FOCUS Too often the communicative approach to learning languages focuses on output rather than input. Intentionally or not, speaking unfortunately often trumps listening. Besides pointing out the obvious that one cannot meaningfully communicate with others without listening, poor listening skills also hinder one's ability to learn more of the language. To help rectify this oft-seen imbalance, this activity, while fully communicative, puts the emphasis on listening.

LEVEL Elementary—Advanced ★ ★ ★

TIME Elementary Activity: 15—20 minutes
Intermediate & Advanced Activity:
20—30 minutes

PROCEDURE

── Elementary Activity ──

01 Depending on group dynamics, either the teacher pairs up students or has each student randomly select a card with their interviewee's name on it. Also, logistics will determine whether interviews would be better conducted in the classroom or as a homework assignment.

02 Help students prepare for the interview by providing sample questions in English. As a class, translate them into Chinese. For example:

- What is your name?

- What is your major?

- What grade/year are you in?

- Do you like studying Chinese? Why?

- How long have you been learning Chinese?

- Do you often practice speaking Chinese?

- Do you often practice listening to Chinese?

- Do you read the texts out loud?

- How often do you speak Chinese and write Chinese characters?

- Who do you usually practice Chinese with?

- Do you have a Chinese friend to practice Chinese with?

- How is your Chinese?

- Do you speak Chinese quickly or slowly?

- Do you write Chinese characters beautifully or just so-so?

While students can make up their own questions for the interview, they should use the vocabulary and sentence patterns that everyone has learned to date.

03 ⟩ Have the students videotape the interview using their phones or some other devices, and then email the teacher the video. If the class has a discussion board, uploading the videos to it and having students comment on the videos is another possibility.

04 ⟩ Have students hand in a written summary of their interview by describing the interviewee based on their answers to the questions raised.

— Intermediate & Advanced Activity —

Even at this stage, don't hesitate to provide students with prepared questions. The students need to concentrate as much as possible on understanding their interviewee. Students will have two challenges. First, students will need to read the questions well enough for native speakers to understand them. Second, the students will have to understand the native speakers well enough to write down what they say. Not easy. If the topic chosen (with the requisite vocabulary and sentence patterns) is beyond your students' current level, then you may simply go over possible questions in class by asking the students what would be appropriate. For more challenging interviews, however, a prepared sheet which you go over in class would be a better approach. *(See Sample.)*

Don't forget though that the key here is to use course content as a jumping off point. For example, the sample shown was for students who had read a piece about the Chinese education system. The interview should reinforce vocabulary and sentence structures that students have already learned, but may have not mastered yet.

01 After you have worked out the logistics and the students have native speakers to interview, a good idea would be to go over some general handy phrases, for example:

- 能不能采访您一下？

- 我想问一些关于高考的问题，可以吗？

- 对不起，我没听清楚，请您再说一遍。

- 能不能把……写下来？

02 When the students have handed in their findings, a relaxed in-class discussion about their interviews works well.

高考采访

1. 高考考哪几门？

2. 为了准备高考，你每天学习多长时间？请谈一谈你的日常学习安排。

3. 父母给你的压力大吗？你是从什么时候开始感觉到有压力的？

4. 高考那天，你紧张吗？

5. 高考结束后，你做了什么？

6. 你考出理想的成绩了吗？

7. 你认为高考改变你的命运了吗？

8. 你觉得高考公平吗？为什么呢？

9. 你认为高考制度有需要改进的地方吗？如果有，你认为该怎么改？

10. 请谈谈你的高考经历。

ACTIVITY
50 **Let's Chat!**

FOCUS Chatting is part of daily life. Now Chinese people chat daily on WeChat, which is a free, fast, and easy-to-use communication tool. If learners of Chinese can utilize the app to practice speaking and writing by chatting with friends, isn't that a great pleasure? By using WeChat, this activity enables students to air their opinions on some interesting topics in a safe and friendly setting, thereby improving their communicative skills.

LEVEL Elementary—Advanced ★ ★ ★

TIME Outside of the classroom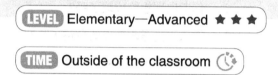

PROCEDURE

— Elementary Activity —

01 Have students download the WeChat app, install it on their smart phones or iPads, and create a WeChat account.

02 If the class is small (six to eight students), create one WeChat Group for the entire class. If the class is larger, create several WeChat Groups with each containing six students or so. Try to group students of similar levels of proficiency together.

03 Develop guidelines for chatting. For example:
a. The group chat should be used solely for learning purposes;
b. Try to participate in the group chats as early as possible because late comers cannot simply "plagiarize" the comments used by others.

04 Each week give the students the weekly chat topic. By all means, ask students for their opinions on possible topics as well. *(See Sample.)*

Require that students drop a few lines either in *pinyin* or characters depending upon their current ability. At times, it might be constructive to ask the students to use specific sentence structures or vocabulary.

05 As the students chat, the teacher should monitor their discussions and make note of errors, so they can be addressed in class. From time to time, it is helpful for the teacher to participate as well.

— Intermediate & Advanced Activity —

01 Find native Chinese speakers who are interested in improving their English and would like to serve as language-exchange partners with your students. Pair up the students based on similar interests.

02 In addition to sending one another text messages, they can also use the video call feature which mimics having a face-to-face conversation.

1. 你的家乡在哪里？

2. 你的爱好是什么？

3. 你的校园生活怎么样？

4. 你会说什么外语？你觉得哪一种语言最难学？

5. 你喜欢什么食物、电影、体育活动和书籍？

6. 谁是你最好的朋友？

7. 你最喜欢哪位老师？

8. 你有工作吗？你喜欢你的工作吗？

9. 你的理想工作是什么？

10. 你喜欢把钱用在哪些地方？

11. 假期你去哪里玩了？

12. 如果你有条件周游世界，最想去什么地方旅游？

References and Further Readings

Chao, Y. R. *A Grammar of Spoken Chinese*. Berkeley: University of California Press, 1968.

Ellis, R. *Task-Based Language Learning and Teaching*. Oxford: Oxford University Press, 2003.

Folse, K. S. *Vocabulary Myths: Applying Second Language Research to Classroom Teaching*. Ann Arbor: The University of Michigan Press, 2004.

Johnson, K. *Designing Language Teaching Tasks*. London: Palgrave Macmillan, 2003.

Lewis, M. & Reinders, H. (eds.). *New Ways in Teaching Adults*. Annapolis Junction, MD: TESOL Press, 1997.

Lightbown, P. M. & Spada, N. *How Languages are Learned (4th Edition)*. Oxford: Oxford University Press, 2013.

Nunan, D. *Designing Tasks for the Communicative Classroom*. Cambridge: Cambridge University Press, 1989.

Slabakova, R. Acquiring Temporal Meanings Without Tense Morphology: The Case of L2 Mandarin Chinese. *The Modern Language Journal*, 2015(2).

Spada, N. & Lightbown, P. M. Form-Focused Instruction: Isolated or Integrated?. *TESOL Quarterly*, 2008(42).

Ur, P. *Grammar Practice Activities: A Practical Guide for Teachers*. Cambridge: Cambridge University Press, 2009.

Wilkins, D. A. *Linguistics in Language Teaching*. London: Edward Arnold, 1972.

Willis, J. *A Framework for Task-Based Learning*. London: Longman, 1996.

Wright, A., Betteridge, D. & Buckby, M. *Games for Language Learning*. Cambridge: Cambridge University Press, 2006.

Xing, J. Z. *Teaching and Learning Chinese as a Foreign Language: A Pedagogical Grammar*. Hong Kong: Hong Kong University Press, 2006.

Yao, T. & McGinnis, S. *Let's Play Games in Chinese*. Boston: Cheng & Tsui Company, 2002.

李德津，程美珍. 外国人实用汉语语法. 北京：华语教学出版社，1988.